COACHING AND LEARNING
TENNIS BASICS

PATRICK DIEGAN

Foreword by John Figaro

ISBN 978-1-4303-0415-9 Published by Lulu.com

CONTENTS

FOREWORD

Passion, when I see it I know it.

No where is it more evident than when watching the writer of this book in action.
I have trained and competed against him on the tennis court, I have seen his tennis brilliance, the results of his coaching, and when you read this book, you too will be able to enjoy and share his passion for the sport of tennis, but more importantly, you will easily teach yourself and others with extreme ease.

Patrick's knowledge of the sport is projected to the reader as if he is next to you on the court giving you instructions whenever you need them. His words, tips and unique approach to the game will stay with you long after you're done reading. In fact, the genius of this book is that you will constantly refer to it in your tennis journey. What you have in your hand is your tennis bible. I greatly enjoyed and highly recommend Patrick's work.

Tennis is as they say the sport of a lifetime, your interest in tennis is the first step, finding and reading "Coaching and Learning Tennis Basics" is the second step. By the time you reach the last chapter you will understand every aspect of the game. With practice, the joy and knowledge of tennis will be yours to use and pass along to your students.

Your tennis life has begun-Enjoy!

John Figaro

Founder of 1st Serve.com the USA's first computer based tennis league.

INTRODUCTION

This tennis book has been written for a number of purposes, foremost of which is to serve as a reference guide that students learning the game can use to support their training. It is the book I couldn't find when developing my tennis as a junior. The book that provides the information you really need to know in a more readable and understandable style without the padding or gloss. The sections on the Forehand, the Backhand and the Service all start with the teaching progressions, ball feeding and self ball feeding techniques I use in a group situation. These same progressions can be used for both child and adult beginners. I go on to show how to introduce topspin and slice on forehand and backhand ground strokes to an individual student as well as the basic teaching progressions on the forehand and backhand Volley.

My system of training sets about giving a student the confidence enhancing means to learn a solid base of stroke, the ability to rally and play the game as quickly as possible. As a coach I am essentially a guide in helping people to learn the game. Development in tennis takes time and how quickly you improve will very much be determined by the hours that you put in and the patience shown. This book sets about enabling you to become your own coach. In tennis you must be equipped with the know how to change things when they are not going well, both in training and on the match court. If some of the tips picked up from this book enter your head at such times then I have succeeded in my quest to help you.

If you are an intermediate or advanced player then check techniques in later sections such as the Advanced Volley; Return of Serve; Approach shot and Speciality Shot sections. Here the goal should be to cut out any unnecessary complications to your own technique. Whatever your level and aims, you will start to derive a real understanding of fundamental tennis technique from these sections. My sections on Beginner, Intermediate, Advanced Singles and Doubles Tactics and Pre-Match Preparation should help enormously before you go out and play your matches. Make sure to review the Fitness section and try and incorporate some of the exercises and routines into your daily training.

I have had the good fortune to train and play tennis in many different parts of the world which has exposed me to trainers and players with many different styles. A good trainer says the right things at the right times and uses plenty of visual demonstrations. He doesn't waste his breath on unnecessary jargon. All written descriptions in this book will relate to right handed players so please reverse the instruction for left handers.

SELECTION OF A RACKET

CHILDREN'S RACKETS

All the leading brands such as Prince, Wilson, Babolat, Fischer, Head, Dunlop and Slazenger provide an excellent range of children's rackets. There are normally 3 grades of children's rackets within each brand.

1. For the age group 4 to 6 are very light, shortest in length at 21 inches and mostly oversize.

2. For the age group 6 to 8 they are again very light, two inches longer at 23 inches and mostly oversize.

3. For the age group 8 to 10, very light, 25 inches in length and mostly oversize. There are also 26 and 26 1/2 inch junior frames available for the taller kids within this age range.

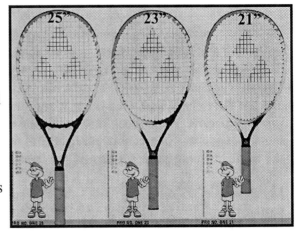

All the above grades have very thin handles (4.0"or grip 0) or less, suitable for the smallest of hands. They are all light and easy to swing. Children within the above age ranges vary significantly in their physical development, so try to let any potential coach see the child before the purchase of the racket.

ADULT RACKETS

1. CHOOSING THE CORRECT GRIP

Grip sizes will be marked in either or both of the following ways. Ranging from smallest to largest we have the following: 4 1/8 or grip 1, 4 1/4 or grip 2, 4 3/8 or grip 3, 4 1/2 or grip 4, 4 5/8 or grip 5. The letters placed infront of the numbers represent the weight, either L=Light, M=Medium, SL=Superlight or XL=Extra Light.

A typical example would be L4 meaning Light, grip size 4.
With the racket placed in the Eastern Forehand or shake hands grip **(see FIG opposite)**, ensure the gap between the finger next to your baby finger and the base area of the thumb is approximately 1cm. Make sure to include an overwrap, thereby allowing for the accompanying growth in grip size.

2. MIDSIZE OR OVERSIZE

Here we become concerned with the hitting area of the hoop. Generally midsize frames are around 90 to 95 square inches and oversize frames 110 square inches and above. The leading manufacturers offer a tremendous range of mid and oversize frames and for an adult beginner the correct selection can prove very difficult. Here I would recommend a thinner beamed lightweight oversize frame. The increased sweet spot or optimum hitting area automatically helps to instill confidence, especially on the volley. Such frames are very maneuverable and excellent for learning the service, particularly the spins. For intermediate and advanced players remember that oversize frames allow for lots of spin and are becoming ever more powerful. For the more accomplished player who has developed his tennis over the years I recommend a midsize heavier frame. This kind of frame will allow both control and power. Players with large swings and fast swing speeds don't need too much extra power in the racket. That power comes from the swing, and so a controllable frame becomes vital. Such players should choose frames 11 ounces and above.

3. EXTRA LONG OR STANDARD

Extra long rackets have now been on the market for many years and have been ever popular since the days of Michael Chang's success when he reached No. 2 with the Prince extra long "Michael Chang Graphite." Extra longs are up to two inches longer than the standard size 27" frame. Their introduction represented the most significant innovation in the racket industry after the Prince oversize in 1976 and the Wilson widebody in 1987. The rackets offer more power off the ground and more reach on the volley. However, it is on the serve that you will get the most help. You will serve from a higher point of elevation, an advantage those six foot plus giants have had over the shorter players over the years. The longer racket opens up a hitting window from which shorter players with weaker serves can now do a lot more than just loop their serves over the net.

4. BEAM, WIDE OR NARROW?

The beam is the width or thickness of the frame viewed from the side. In general a wider beam is stiff and powerful, while a thinner beam is more flexible with a cushioned response.

Contoured beam Here the beam varies in dimension from tip to grip. Many wide bodied designs feature contoured or sculpted beams with areas that are wider and stiffer for more power. Such areas are combined with thinner portions of the frame that are more flexible or cushioned for enhanced playing comfort.

Constant tapered beam Here the beam widens or slims uniformly from tip to shoulders. Thin shafted rackets with broad and stiff hoops offer power with a cushioned response while thinner hoops and thicker shafted frames are quick with a quick shot response.

Dual tapered beam This is thinner through the handle and shaft, thickest at the shoulders and thins again through the hoop and tip. This design provides for enhanced stability on mishits and a solid, powerful shot response.

5. HEAD LIGHT OR HEAD HEAVY?

When selecting a racket try to determine where the weight of the frame is distributed. Is it head light or head heavy or more of an even distribution? Head light rackets have more weight near the lower half or handle end and are generally more maneuverable. They are best suited to doubles or serve volleyers in singles. They are, however, more likely to twist in your hand when shots are hit off center. Head heavy rackets have more weight in the top half and are generally more powerful. They are generally more suited to players with smooth, full strokes, advanced players and back court specialists. By balancing the center of the racket on your index finger you can determine the weight distribution of the racket.

KNOWING YOUR GRIPS

Grips vary significantly from stroke to stroke and player to player. Racket handles are different and hand shapes differ so that each type of grip will fit slightly differently for each player. Let us now take a look at the most common grip types.

1. EASTERN FOREHAND GRIP

Here the "V" formed between the index finger and the thumb rests somewhere on the middle of the top panel to the upper side of the top right bevel. The grip can be achieved by simply "shaking hands" with the racket whilst held in an edgeways position.

Advantages:

A) It is a good grip for all surfaces, good for handling inside and outside balls and balls of varying heights.

B) The grip presents a vertical racket face to the ball necessary for good topspin development.

C) It offers a solid comfortable grip for beginners giving an overall feeling of strength because of the hand
   Support.

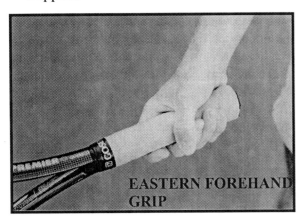

EASTERN FOREHAND GRIP

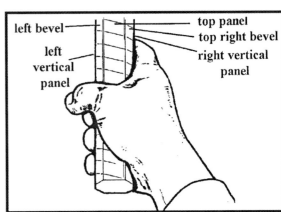

2. EASTERN BACKHAND GRIP

Here the "V" formed between the thumb and the index finger rests toward the bottom of the top left bevel. Find the grip by turning the hand a 1/4 turn inward from the Eastern Forehand grip. This is the basic one handed grip in tennis, good for all surfaces and good for topspin and slice.

Advantages:

A) It is a good grip for inside and outside balls of varying heights.

B) It presents a vertical racket face to the ball ideal for good topspin development.

C) It is a good grip for beginners giving an overall feeling of hand support.

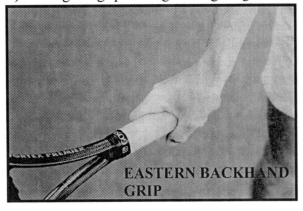

EASTERN BACKHAND GRIP

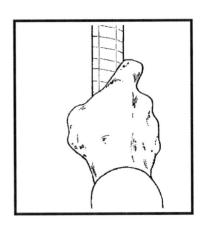

8

3. THE CONTINENTAL OR "CHOPPER" GRIP

The "V" rests towards the top of the top left bevel. The heel of the hand covers the top panel. With a Semi Continental the heel of the hand covers half of the top panel. You can find this grip by holding the racket edgeways and wielding the racket in a chopping motion.

Advantages:

A) The grip can be used for all shots.

B) It is an excellent grip for volleys where there is often no time to make a grip change, particularly during fast volley exchanges.

C) It offers versatility on low and sliced balls which call for an open racket face.

Disadvantages:

A) Handling high balls on the forehand side becomes difficult, where a very strong wrist and excellent timing is required in order to control the racket face.

B) The grip makes the development of a topspin backhand more difficult, due to the lack of behind the racket feel and equal wrist stability compared to the Eastern Backhand grip.

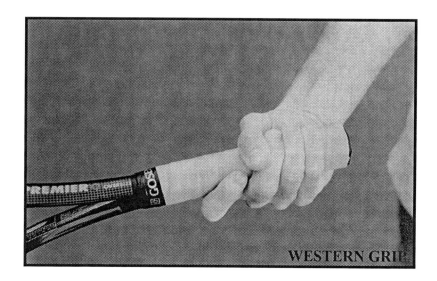

CONTINENTAL GRIP

WESTERN GRIP

4. THE SEMI-WESTERN GRIP

Here the "V" formed between the index finger and the thumb rests toward the middle of the bottom of the top right bevel. The grip makes for a closed racket face and is well suited to topspin.

5. THE WESTERN GRIP

Here the "V" formed between the index finger and the thumb rests towards the middle of the right vertical panel. You can find the grip by placing the hand beneath the edgeways facing racket. The grip originated on the high bouncing courts of California where the ball bounces mostly waist high and above.

Advantages:

A) The grip makes for a closed racket face on contact giving a great deal of topspin.

B) The same grip can be used to hit excessive topspin off both sides by using the same face of racket.

Disadvantages:

A) Low and sliced balls are difficult to hit because it is difficult to rotate the wrist sufficiently and open the racket face.

B) The use of the same excessive grip for both forehand and backhand places a tremendous stress load on the arm.

6. TWO HANDED BACKHAND GRIPS

A) 2 EASTERN FOREHANDS
Here the top hand is the more dominant.
This is an excellent grip for beginners, both palms behind the handle providing a great deal of stability. As soon as the backhand becomes reasonably sound, it is better to move the student to a grip with the Eastern Forehand continuing on the top, but a Continental grip on the bottom. If after continued prompting the beginner continues to feel uncomfortable with this grip then let him stay with the first grip. The main advantage of the second grip is that when hitting one handed sliced backhands no grip change is required.

B) 1 CONTINENTAL GRIP (BOTTOM HAND) AND 1 EASTERN FOREHAND GRIP (TOP HAND)
As mentioned above. With this grip either or neither hand may be the more dominant.

C) 1 EASTERN BACKHAND GRIP (BOTTOM HAND) AND 1 EASTERN FOREHAND (TOP HAND)
The bottom hand is more dominant. The racket face will be more naturally closed on impact due to the backhand grip. This is an excellent grip for developing topspin and slice.

D) 1 EASTERN BACKHAND GRIP, FULL (BOTTOM HAND) AND 1 SEMI-WESTERN FOREHAND GRIP (TOP HAND)
Either or neither hand may be the more dominant. The resulting closed racket face will again create excessive topspin. When hitting a slice both hands have to be re-positioned, the bottom hand less extreme and the top hand more towards an Eastern Forehand.

7. SEMI-TWO HANDER
All the above grips may be used for this type of stroke where the top hand is released on contact with the ball. An aggressive snapping away of the left wrist and accompanying acceleration of the racket hand together can create terrific topspin and power.

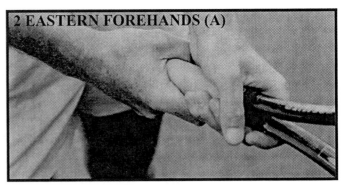

2 EASTERN FOREHANDS (A)

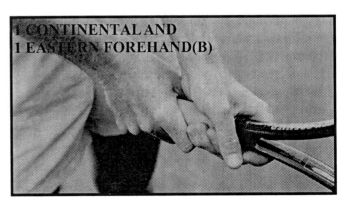

1 CONTINENTAL AND 1 EASTERN FOREHAND (B)

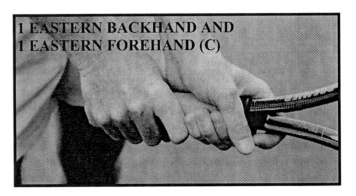

1 EASTERN BACKHAND AND 1 EASTERN FOREHAND (C)

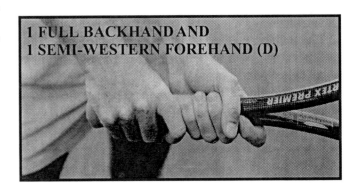

1 FULL BACKHAND AND 1 SEMI-WESTERN FOREHAND (D)

THE FOREHAND

INTRODUCTION

Remember that when teaching a group of beginner students there is often going to be a wide disparity of ability across the group and from group to group. This all depends on a variety of factors such as age, size, strength, natural ability and pre-existing ideas on how to hit a tennis ball. There is no one best way to teach a beginner group although some methods are definitely more efficient than others. The methods I use offer a great deal of flexibility in terms of catering to all ability levels. Use good judgment, common sense and progressions and practices to match the overall requirements of the group. Always remember that the end goal is to get them rallying and playing the game as quickly as possible because it's here that the real fun begins. Let's take a look at some of the progressions and practices involved when teaching a group of beginner children. These methods can be incorporated into adult group teaching also. The order of the sequence of the progressions is a good indicator of the general order I would use as the students progress in skill level, an order not restricted to any particular time period. Gradually and subtly increase the difficulty of the practices and progressions. Ensure that students satisfactorily master the necessary technique in each progression and practice before moving on to the next.

DEMONSTRATING THE FOREHAND

From the service line demonstrate some neutral stance forehand drives with a very short backswing, the racket taken back just behind and below the back hip. Demonstrate both a medium follow through (halfway between the point of contact and full follow through) as shown in **(PHOTO 1)** and full follow through **(PHOTO 4)**. Move back to the baseline and demonstrate with a full backswing **(PHOTO 2)** and follow through. Also demonstrate some drives from an open stance hitting position **(See PHOTOS 11&14 page 22)**. The full elevated follow through as shown in **(PHOTO 4)** may also finish with the elbow more bent, the racket all the way over the shoulder. Make it clear to the students that the size of the backswing is often governed by how close they are to the net and the speed of the oncoming ball. Also emphasise that the position of the feet as already demonstrated can be set in different positions to hit the tennis ball.

INTRODUCING THE GRIP

Introduce to each student an Eastern Forehand grip, ensuring hands are placed nicely behind the racket handles.

PHOTO 1

PHOTO 2

Backswing

PHOTO 3

Contact

PHOTO 4

Follow through

11

DROP FEEDING

Move the students close up to the net and in their sideways standing positions drop feed some balls to each in turn. In this neutral stance position each student can become quickly acquainted with a simple linear back foot to front foot weight transfer and most importantly good balance. Have each student edge the racket forwards without a backswing. The contact position should be comfortably to the side and just in front of the front hip. On contact have them open the racket face and clear the net straight ahead. As an addition to this exercise have them move a little further back, feed from in front and have them edge the racket ahead so that you may catch the ball in front of them **(PHOTO 5).** Move the students back to the service line or just inside, and continuing to drop feed them **(PHOTO 6),** have them play a straight ahead forehand with a very short backswing and medium follow through. Ensure that their rackets stay straight on contact, travel on a low to high path and that they take a short step ahead as they take their rackets back.

Give the students plenty of time to practice self feeding off their own ball drop. Demonstrate a self feed with a very short backswing and medium follow through. Indicate a good contact position for a straight ahead drive, comfortably to the side, around waist level and in front of the front hip. Introduce cones for target practice and competitions for the most accurate hitting.

CLOSE CONTACT RALLYING (PHOTO 7)

Introduce plenty of close contact rallying with the students where the focus is on contact and the ball is effectively tapped back and forth, forehand to forehand, racket faces open to sustain the rally.

12

Give the students plenty of time to practice close contact rallying with each other **(PHOTO 8)**.

PHOTO 8

HAND FEEDING FROM IN FRONT

Begin with plenty of feeding to the sideways standing students, yourself positioned on their side of the net. Proceed to demonstrate to the students a correct hand feed. Show how a slow underarm movement with late ball release gives the hitter plenty of time to swing at the ball. Show how the position of the ball should be comfortably to the side of the hitter, and also that the ball should bounce well in front so that the hitter can hit the easier falling ball on arrival. A racket cover can be placed at the best bounce point, the feeders aiming to make their feeds bounce in line with this guide. Let the students practice themselves **(PHOTO 9)**.

READY POSITION

With their balance and swings really starting to shape up move them into a forwards facing ready position to receive your feeds **(PHOTO 10)**. Here the feet should be shoulder width apart, the knees bent, body weight forward on the balls of the feet. The racket should be held directly in front or slightly to the backhand side, the bottom hand in an Eastern Forehand grip, the top hand in an Eastern position right next to it. Begin feeding and ensure they are using very short backswings and now over the shoulder follow throughs. When they hit neutral stance ensure that they pivot out right with their right feet with the shoulder turn (unit turn). Introduce open stance hitting **(PHOTO 11)** and ensure that when their right feet move out right that on landing they also pivot right. Ensure that their left knees bend to enable their hips to turn sideways. Ensure that they are all making a good angular (rotational) weight transfer to the right foot before re-shifting back to the left.

PHOTO 9

PHOTO 10

PHOTO 11

13

RACKET FEEDING FROM ACROSS THE NET

Move your feeding position to the other side of the net and proceed to racket feed **(PHOTO 12)**. Continue to have the students hit with very short backswings and full follow throughs. As the students become more proficient move them back toward the baseline gradually allowing them to increase the length of their backswings. Get them to the stage where they can play forehands with full backswings and follow throughs from the baseline with solid looking strokes.

PHOTO 12

HITTING ON THE MOVE

As technique improves the time becomes right for more challenging movement patterns.

1. Walking across the court and back

Line up the students outside the court near the service line, the hitter in a sideways position at the junction between the service line and the singles side line ready to go. Have each student walk slowly across the court along the service line and feed balls set away giving sufficient time to make a good ball contact and full follow through. Ensure that backswings stay very short. Have the students walk backwards and do the same.

2. Moving to the ball and side stepping back to position

Give each student two balls set away giving time to make some steps to the ball before hitting and side shuffling back. Ensure that each student stops when he gets to the ball and makes a balanced shot with good spacing between himself and the ball.

3. Side shuffle and step

Feed each student two balls, the first positioned far enough to the side to make a side shuffle and hit before a side-shuffle back to be ready for the next. Work on both neutral stance and open stance hitting here.

4. Running and hitting

With the students gaining in competence move them back to just inside the baseline and have them practice running and hitting three ball feeds across. Let them try lengthening their backswings but make sure that their swings are staying reasonably sound and that they are maintaining a good comfortable distance between themselves and the ball. When they feel well set encourage them to use full over the shoulder follow throughs.

THE TWO HANDED FOREHAND

Use a two handed forehand for the very young kids and the weaker wristed students in the beginning stages. This will help to instill confidence and racket stability in the earliest stages of learning the swing. For a right hander the right hand will go on top of the handle in an Eastern Forehand position, the left hand also in an Eastern on the bottom.

THE ONE BOX DRILL

This is a really good drill for beginners. Here the paired off students stand on opposite sides of the net in one service box. One ball is used between both players. The object is to throw the ball into the opponent's box forcing him to miss the catch **(PHOTO 13)**.

The following rules must be made clear to make the game effective.
1. A point is lost when the ball is thrown into the net or not caught in one or both hands by the receiver after the bounce **2.** The point is also lost if the ball is caught without bouncing **3.** Serve alternately point by point, throughout the game and from outside the service box. The winner is the first to 11 points **4.** The receiver can stand anywhere inside or outside their service box and must throw the ball from where they catch it **5.** The rally will continue in this way until one person makes a mistake or is beaten by a winner **6.** Balls may be thrown either over arm or under arm.

Make sure to make the following clear to students playing this game.
1. The importance of standing in a good position.
2. Learning to leave balls which are going out.
3. Responding to high balls by moving quickly back and low balls by moving quickly forwards.
4. Placing the ball away from the opponent.
5. Learning when the time is right for the killer throw.
6. Learning when the time is right for the soft throw.

MINI TENNIS

The throwing game leads nicely into mini tennis, now both players using a racket. One bounce self feeds may be used or mini over arm serves to start the rallies. Both the throwing game and mini tennis can be introduced in the earliest stages and are ideal for learning court positioning, spatial awareness, ball control and the ability to rally.

PHOTO 13

FOREHAND DRIVE: COMMON FAULTS AND CURES

FAULT 1 Excessive backswing.
CURE 1 While drop feeding to the student place a plastic chair behind, so that if the racket head is drawn back too much it will hit the chair.
CURE 2 Use your racket as a stopper while the student feeds himself.

FAULT 2 Backswing always too short.
CURE Encourage the student to hide the racket from the forwards feeding coach.

FAULT 3 Inadequate follow through.
CURE Request the student to hit a few balls over the net without a backswing.

FAULT 4 Exaggerated follow through.
CURE 1 Stop at the point of contact and then add the follow through.
CURE 2 Have the student stand with the fence directly to his left and toss a few balls until the racket no longer hits the fence.

FAULT 5 Follow through not finishing high enough.
CURE Encourage the student to catch the racket in the non-playing hand up high when across the left Shoulder.

FAULT 6 Loose wrist on contact.
CURE 1 Encourage the student to squeeze his fingers lightly on the contact.
CURE 2 Request that the student hold the racket higher up the handle.

FAULT 7 Trunk and shoulders not rotating sufficiently through the hit.
CURE Again, catching the racket in the non-playing hand will help to cure this problem.

FOOTWORK, MOVEMENT AND RECOVERY PRIORITIES

INTRODUCTION

As a student develops over time and the stroke technique becomes more automated you must bring in the following movement patterns. Trust your own judgement here and always remember the importance of developing a well balanced player with strokes that will hold up to any kind of ball given.

THE SPLIT STEP

Explain to the student that every time their hitting partner or opponent is about to make contact they must get into the habit of split stepping **(See fig below)** whereby he takes a quick hop off the ground, both feet landing slightly further apart from where they started. This will give him the means of moving much more quickly in any direction. Train the student to keep on the balls of his feet at all times when a rally is in progress. Some players might prefer to hop from one foot to another very quickly to keep the feet activated, others prefer to rest on the balls of their feet in order to stay springy with the knees acting like shock absorbers.

SPLIT STEP

THE SIDE SHUFFLE AND RECOVERY STEP

Teach the student the movement of a side shuffle and step to handle moderately paced balls directed within about 6 feet either side of center. The side shuffle and step on the forehand side is initiated after the split step is landed with both feet again coming off the ground. Here the inside foot (left foot) slides up to the outside foot, (right foot) and almost touches it before the outside foot moves out to the right. When the outside foot for a neutral or closed stance forehand lands it pivots out to the right enabling the left foot to lead ahead or across into the stroke. On the backhand side the reverse takes place with the right foot finally stepping forwards and across into the swing. On the forehand the back foot should come around into a position parallel to the left to enable a forwards facing ready position and recovery. On the backhand it is the left foot that comes around.

MOVING BACK BEHIND THE BALL

For this type of ball teach the student to turn early to the side that the ball is coming and slide back using a sideways on side-shuffling movement. This type of ball might have to be played after moving forward to play a shorter ball or a high topspin ball that drives the player well behind the baseline. After sliding back the player must come off the ground with both feet in synchronisation with the forward swing. This enables the body to swing around and return to a net facing position and recover. For the type of high topspin ball that takes the player close up to the back fence teach a reverse pivot movement. Here the student comes off the ground with the forward swing, swings around and ends up facing opposite to the side he slid back on. These techniques give the player the means to stay on the offensive even when moving backwards and a well balanced recovery.

THE OPEN STANCE CROSS OVER RECOVERY STEP

When forced wide teach the student to recover by crossing the outside leg over the inside before side shuffling back to a balanced court position. This movement should be used on both open stance forehands and backhands.

THE OPEN STANCE OUT-STEP

Teach the student an out-step technique when playing open stance forehands and backhands on wider balls where there is already some momentum moving sideways to the ball. Here the outside foot should come off the ground and move more to the outside in synchronization with the forward swing to contact. This recovery step (break step) greatly helps a more balanced angular (rotational) weight transfer through the stroke when moving to the right or left, particularly at speed. It allows an uncoiling of the hips and enables a much faster recovery. The inside foot will come off the ground as the body weight shifts on to the outside foot which will in turn leave the ground just before contact.

RECOVERING FROM RUNNING AT SPEED

When trying to recover after running for a very wide ball teach the student a large recovery step (breakstep) where after the front foot steps across and into the shot, the back foot swings around parallel to the front foot in synchronization with the end of the follow through. This enables a recovery back to cover the middle of the court or a sprint back to the other side.

RUN AROUND FOREHAND

When a player runs around his backhand to play a forehand the sideways momentum will be right to left. Therefore a pronounced right left weight transfer will occur which often leads to an outstep (breakstep) of the left foot instead of the right.

MOVEMENT DRILL

One particularly good drill that can really test various types of movement is as follows. Stand with a basket of balls close to the net on the same side of the court as the student who should be positioned on the baseline **(FIG 1)**. Any balls hit by the student must be down the line. First, test the student by feeding an underarm feed high and deep. Then alternate with a ball landing at the baseline around waist height. Make sure that the student turns to the side and slides back behind the first feed before hitting and returning to the baseline. Work both sides before alternating backhands and forehands. Next you could add short balls to the sequence. This is the perfect drill for recovery behind the ball and the reverse pivot recovery step. A mixed sequence could be added and, later, wider and shorter angled balls could be thrown in. Use a similar drill **(FIG 2)** to test each student on far and wide balls making sure that the outside foot is crossed over the inside for a quick recovery. These can be mixed with less wide balls and alternated. Your position of feeding should change to the alley to enable the student to hit cross court here. This is perfect for teaching the outstep technique.

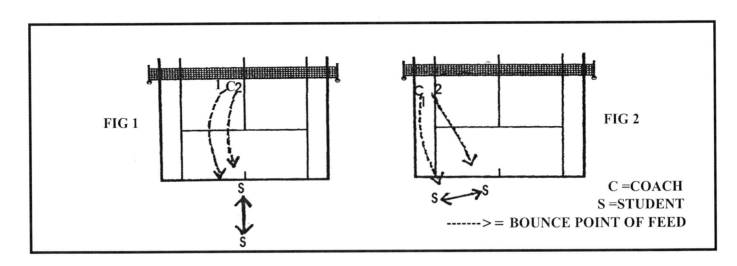

FIG 1   FIG 2

C = COACH
S = STUDENT
------> = BOUNCE POINT OF FEED

INTRODUCTION TO TOPSPIN

Topspin is generated when the top surface of the tennis ball rotates against air resistance. This resistance creates friction and therefore pressure which forces the ball down. The degree of topspin and subsequent arc in flight of the ball will greatly effect the ball's bounce. An excessively topspun ball will approach the court at a very steep angle and will therefore bounce very high, although the amount of height and the accompanying bound forward or kick will very much be affected by the court surface. The ball will bite into a rough textured surface such as red clay making the bounce and kick severe. However, on a smooth textured surface such as grass or fast hard little resistance is offered and so the ball will tend to shoot through and stay very low.

All today's tour players hit with topspin off the ground, many with extreme topspin due to Semi-Western and Western grips on the forehand and aggressive single and double handed backhands. If you are going to reach a high level in tennis you have to learn it. The very fast swing speeds of today's players and high tech rackets are giving ever increasing speed and topspin to the ball. Tactically this means that you can hit with real power, but with control at the same time. It provides safety with its high clearance over the net and even if your ball lands short, the resultant kick will provide you protection from attack. It provides options in both attack and defense. You can keep your opponent pinned to the baseline with deep topspin drives or topspin lobs. I will now go on to show how I would introduce topspin in an individual teaching situation.

James Blake

INTRODUCING THE TOPSPIN FOREHAND

The following descriptions will relate to the individual situation. With the development of a good lifted forehand the ball should already be rotating forwards slightly on its flight path, the introduction of topspin is a natural progression from this stage. Urge the student with an Eastern Forehand grip to come a little more under the racket handle to either a position between Eastern and Semi-Western or Semi-Western. He should be able to create good topspin with the Eastern, however, the above grips will directly close the racket face and when in conjunction with the correct swing path will automatically help to create more topspin.

PHOTO 1

PHOTO 2

PHOTO 3

PHOTO 4

If the student is having difficulty producing enough topspin with the Eastern then a closing of the racket face down toward the ground at the beginning of the swing is normally effective. The following steps should now be followed.

1. Move the student to the net and have him place his racket alongside the net band, the ball trapped in between **(PHOTO 1 AND PHOTO 2)**. Instruct him to lift his racket up the back of the trapped ball. The forwards rotating ball should then simply drop over the other side of the net.
2. Move to a position 5 or 6 feet behind the net and now demonstrate a drop feed starting with your racket hand very low. Brush your hand up the back of the ball in the same motion used in the above technique. Keep the follow through medium **(PHOTOS 3&4)**.

Demonstrate from neutral and open stance foot positions. Make sure both stances are practiced when you drop feed him and when he self feeds.

3. Now drop feed to the student and work on this technique **(PHOTOS 5&6)**.

4. Next give plenty of time to let him drop feed himself and perfect it.

5. Move to the service line and demonstrate a swing with the racket arm snapping up above the right shoulder, the ball first bouncing on your side of the net before continuing across it **(PHOTO 7)**.

6. Give him plenty of time to practice this technique, ensuring a good vertical movement of the racket face and a lot of topspin.

7. Working again from the service line demonstrate a topspin drive, this time hitting directly over the net. The racket should now be moving more than just vertically, it must also be moving forwards through the swing.

8. Again, with him feeding himself, have him try the same and give him plenty of time to practice **(PHOTOS 8,9,10)**. Khalid is using a Semi-Western grip and consequently we start working on a more around the body follow through as seen in **PHOTO 10**. Emphasize on the balls high clearance over the net and how the ball kicks forwards on its bounce. Make sure the student understands the importance of this effect on the ball, particularly the tactical advantages. Give some hand feeds from in front and some racket feeds across the net gradually moving him back to the baseline as his competency improves. Practice rallying both on the mini court and the full court, using all stances, including semi-open **(SEE PHOTO 15 OVER PAGE)**.

PHOTO 5

PHOTO 6

PHOTO 7

PHOTO 8

PHOTO 9

PHOTO 10

21

INTRODUCING THE SEMI AND FULL LOOP BACKSWINGS AND THE OPEN AND SEMI-OPEN STANCE FOOT POSITIONS

As the student becomes familiar with the concept and feel for topspin the time becomes right for the introduction of the "semi"or "full"loop into the swing **(SEE PHOTO 11 FULL & PHOTO 12 SEMI).** As with the straight back backswing the swing should start from close to hip level. This time the swing traces a reverse 'C' movement. The larger the movement the more full the loop. In both instances the looping will help develop rhythm and racket speed ideal for the production of topspin. If the student prefers a straight back backswing this is fine.

WHAT STANCE ?

Note the position of my feet in **(PHOTO 11).** They are now in an open stance as I get set to hit my topspin forehand. My body weight has transferred to my right leg which sets me in perfect balance before the forward swing. I have made an angular (rotational) weight transfer, from left to right across my body. Open stance and semi-open stance forehands are geared perfectly for the production of topspin particularly on hard courts. Here frequently high contact positions are made often off fast and high balls where you are in need of a quick recovery.

In **(PHOTO 12)** I'm using a neutral stance to hit my forehand. Here I was crowded and had to get quickly to the side of the ball. I am making more of a linear weight transfer, i.e. from my back foot to my front foot. If I was forced out wide and was on the run I might be forced to play the forehand with a cross over step of the left foot. Here the left foot would cross over the right landing well ahead and firmly on the ground before the forward swing **(PHOTO 13).** In **PHOTOS 14, 15** and **16** Roger Federer displays in order his awesome forehand from open, semi-open and neutral stance hitting positions. He is a master at playing his forehand well with any stance from anywhere in the court. Make sure to introduce all types of footwork when teaching the forehand drive. Even in the earliest stages of rallying on the mini court you can guide the students into hitting with open and semi-open stances. Remember that during the introduction to topspin on the forehand the same teaching steps can be demonstrated and practiced from an open and semi-open stance position. For the open stance instead of stepping ahead with the left foot the right foot can step out to the right and once landed, the forehand swing can begin. Tennis players should have knowledge and awareness of the various types of footwork on the forehand and most importantly how to recover correctly from each. They will subsequently be better able to react to what they receive and also open up more options for themselves.

PHOTO 11

PHOTO 12

PHOTO 13

PHOTO 14

PHOTO 15

PHOTO 16

OLD STYLE FOREHAND COMPARED TO THE MODERN

With the old style or "unit Turn" forehand the racket is generally moved backward in combination with the shoulder turn, the arm rotated entirely about the shoulder. However, the use of the Semi Western and Western grips has led directly to a change in the swing pattern. The grip has now become the determining factor on the type of forehand provided. The swing is now characterized by movement of the elbow backward in combination with, or prior to the shoulder turn and the arm is rotated around the elbow and shoulder. The latter technique provides potential for increased racket speed and therefore increased power. The grips provide the closed racket face necessary for more topspin and control. **(Please refer to the photo sequences on pages 24 & 25)**

PREPARATION PHASE (PHOTOS 1 & 2)
Preparation commences with a bending of the knees. The rear or right foot pivots, the right elbow is moved backward and the shoulders are rotated. All three players have full looped backswings. The left hand remains on the racket initially which assists in the shoulder rotation. The racket face remains closed throughout the backswing as a consequence of the grip.

FORWARD SWING TO CONTACT (PHOTOS 3&4)
As the right or outside foot is planted the forward swing begins. The forward swing commences at the top of the loop, accelerating extremely fast on its path under the ball and up and through. The racket arm stays loose and very relaxed. In the early forward swing the elbow of the right arm is maintained relatively close to the body for stroke stability. The low to high path of the racket increases immediately before contact. The hips, trunk and shoulders rotate forward to a position essentially parallel to the net at contact. The key features of the contact point are that the racket face angle is vertical to the ground and the wrist is laid back as a result of the grip. Contact occurs forward of the right shoulder and is relatively further forward for the cross court compared to the down the line stroke. The head remains stationary and the eyes are focused on the contact region, usually somewhat forward of actual contact.

FOLLOW THROUGH (PHOTOS 5&6)
A good follow through is critical to the direction of the ball, but is also important for the deceleration of the arm. Because Henin-Hardenne is returning a deeper ball and she is rushed her follow through is truncated and finishes higher than the other two players. Keurten and Roddick have more of the windshield wiper motion that requires tremendous wrist strength and flexibility. This inverted around the body follow through is typical of today's tour players with their grips anywhere between Eastern and Semi-Western, Semi-western and Western.

ANDRE AGASSI

23

1
2
3
GUSTAVO KEURTEN

1
2
3
ANDY RODDICK

1
2
3
JUSTINE HENIN -HARDENNE

4   5   6

4   5   6

4   5   6

THE BACKHAND

INTRODUCTION

The Eastern Backhand grip is best for beginners wishing to hit a one handed backhand. Normally it is better to start the weaker wristed beginners such as very young children with a two-handed grip, a Continental for the bottom or lead hand and an Eastern Forehand for the top. Some students may find the Continental grip uncomfortable and prefer two forehand or "slap on" grips. The process of lining up the students, making the relevant demonstrations and feeding progressions remains the same as for the forehand drive. Remember to start ball feeding in the neutral stance sideways position as shown in the photo below. Move on to closed stance backhands and build in the recovery step. Introduce open stance backhands when the time is right. When waiting to receive feeds from the forwards facing ready position for the one-handed backhand, the student should prepare a little differently. Instead of the racket pointing directly ahead, the racket should be held in an Eastern Backhand grip, angled naturally toward the backhand side. The fingers of the left hand should support the racket lightly at the neck.

PHOTO 1

ONE-HANDED OR TWO-HANDED ?

Both the one-handed and two-handed backhands have various pros and cons when compared to each other and below I list some of the more notable ones. As a student develops his tennis the coach should become increasingly aware of whether to guide the student with one or two hands. Very often the one-hander will come naturally to a student and the two-hander will seem very uncomfortable. Other times the two-hander will be the stroke that comes naturally, often this due to lack of sufficient strength.

THE TWO HANDER

1. Both hands on the racket help to give more stability at impact, particularly on service returns. 2. It is easier to develop a topspin backhand with two hands. 3. It is easier to disguise your shots with two hands, and also to create better angles. 4. The second hand is particularly useful for control on the topspin lob, allowing you to brush up the ball more quickly and with more force. 5. The second hand gives you added support when taking balls early or on the rise.

THE ONE HANDER

1. With the one-hander you don't have to be quite as precise on positioning with running shots due to the added reach, particularly when running down drop shots and hitting running passes. 2. It offers far more in terms of flexibility on approach shots, the slice coming more naturally. 3. It is easier to handle low balls with the one-hander.

FOR THE ONE HANDED BACKHAND

PHOTO 2

PHOTO 3

From the service line demonstrate some neutral stance one handed backhand drives with a very short backswing. Start the swing from a racket position in front of the front foot to a position where the racket hand is above the back foot (below hip level). Demonstrate a medium follow through (halfway between point of contact **(PHOTO 3)** and full follow through **(PHOTO 4)**. Also demonstrate with a full follow through. Move back to the baseline and demonstrate with a full backswing and full follow through. Again make it clear that with both one handed and two handed backhands the size of the backswing is often governed by how close the students are to the net and the speed of the oncoming ball. Let us take a look at the demonstration of the one handed backhand in **PHOTOS 2, 3 and 4**.

Note:

A) A full shoulder turn with the racket taken straight back and down, the elbow pushed down maintaining a relatively straight arm on the backswing. As the racket starts to point to the back fence behind the wrist is laid back, the butt of the handle pointing toward the left net post ahead. Indicate how the fingers of the non-playing hand support the throat of the racket as it is taken back and also at the end of the backswing. Body weight shifts to the back foot. **(PHOTO 2)**

B) Step ahead with the right leg. As the front foot hits the ground the forward swing can begin.

C) As the racket comes through to contact the left arm is left behind and points to the back fence behind. The top edge of the racket is above the level of the wrist on contact and well in front of the right leg. Body weight shifts to the front foot; eyes are focused on the contact area. **(PHOTO 3)**

D) The trunk, hips and shoulders rotate into the hit and finish turned 3/4 toward the net. Note the full extension on the follow through, the racket face should be closed over at the very end. Body weight has fully shifted onto the front foot. **(PHOTO 4)**

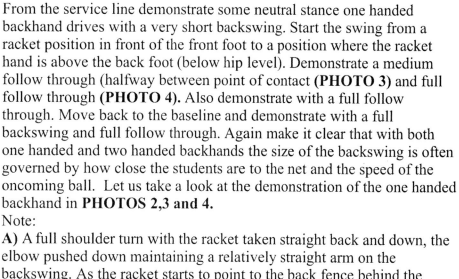

PHOTO 4

FOR THE TWO-HANDED BACKHAND

PHOTO 5

From the service line demonstrate some neutral stance two handed backhand drives with a very short backswing, the racket taken back just behind and below the back hip. Demonstrate a medium follow through (halfway between the point of contact, **PHOTO 6** and full follow through, **PHOTO 7**). Also demonstrate with a full follow through. Move back to the baseline and demonstrate a two handed drive with a full backswing and follow through. Remember to demonstrate some drives from closed and also open stance hitting positions. The students need to know that the feet can be set in different positions to hit the tennis ball. Let us take a look at the demonstration of the two handed drive in **PHOTOS 5,6 and 7**.
Note:
A) The left arm draws the racket back by bending at the elbow, taking it to a position pointing to the back fence **(PHOTO 5)**. The wrists should then be laid back, the shoulders well turned with the head looking over the shoulder at the oncoming ball. The right leg steps ahead. As the front foot hits the ground, the forward swing can begin.
B) The forward swing to contact should follow a low to high path and at contact the racket must be straight, the top edge of the racket above the level of the wrists. The contact position should be ahead of the right front hip **(PHOTO 6)**.
C) On the follow through both arms come up together before bending at shoulder level and carrying the racket behind the right shoulder. Similarly to the forehand the shoulders, belly and trunk should make a full rotation finishing with the body facing the net. Body weight must transfer from the back foot through the forward swing, contact and follow through to the front foot **(PHOTO 7)**.

PHOTO 6

PHOTO 7

ONE-HANDED BACKHAND: COMMON FAULTS AND CURES

FAULT 1 The arm bends too much at the elbow leading to an uncontrolled excessively high racket on the backswing.
CURE Make sure the elbow is pushed down low with only a slight arm bend as the racket is drawn back.

FAULT 2 The racket is not finishing high enough on the follow through.
CURE Encourage the student to expose his right armpit toward a right net post facing position at the end of the follow through.

FAULT 3 The racket is taken back without the support of the left hand.
CURE Ensure that the racket is gripped at the throat with the fingers and guided back by them into a sound backswing position.

FAULT 4 The fingers are bunched together with no gap between the index finger and the rest.
CURE Ensure a spread of the index finger between it and the others.

TWO-HANDED BACKHAND DRIVE: COMMON FAULTS AND CURES

FAULT 1 The right hand is placed at the top of the grip instead of the bottom.
CURE Simply cross the hands back over to the correct positions.

FAULT 2 Hands are too far apart along the handle.
CURE Ensure that both hands are comfortably next to each other, the index finger spread on the lead hand.

FAULT 3 Inadequate shoulder turn.
CURE The cross step and shoulder turn need to be more exaggerated on the two hander. Again, when setting up for the shot, you should be looking over your shoulder at the ball infront of you.

FAULT 4 The Racket finishes forwards only on the follow through.
CURE Ensure the racket flows freely with both elbows bending at shoulder level, taking the racket onwards above the right shoulder.

INTRODUCING THE TOPSPIN BACKHAND

Develop the topspin backhand like the topspin forehand as a natural progression forwards from the basic lifted drives. Now take the following steps:

1. Use the net band demonstration to give a feel for the motion of topspin either one or two handed depending on what you are teaching **(PHOTOS 1&2).**

PHOTO 1   PHOTO 2

2. Move five or six feet behind the net and demonstrate one and two handed drop feeds. If you are teaching a one handed backhand, drop your racket hand low and brush up the back of the ball making sure to keep the wrist firm. Again keep the backswing and follow through much more limited than normal **(PHOTO 3).** When demonstrating a two handed backhand, drop both racket hands and snap up with the wrists at the same time as the racket head comes upwards **(PHOTO 4).**

3. Proceed to drop feed the student **(PHOTOS 5&6).**

4. Now give him plenty of time to practice self feeding using the above technique.

5. Move back to the service line and demonstrate the one handed swing with the elbow snapping upwards, the racket finishing over the right shoulder **(PHOTO 7).** On the two hander both elbows should snap upwards **(PHOTO 8).** The ball must bounce on your side of the court before continuing over the net.

PHOTO 3   PHOTO 4

6. Direct the student to feed to himself with high bouncing self feeds and practice this exercise.

7. Now demonstrate hitting directly over the net, not just vertically, but at the same time forward through the swing. The follow through should now take on a more natural look, but on the one hander much higher at the end.

8. Have him drop feed to himself and practice the same.

9. Proceed to make the same feeding progressions as for the topspin forehand.

PHOTO 5   PHOTO 6

PHOTO 7   PHOTO 8

ONE-HANDED BACKHAND-MODERN STYLE

THE GRIP-Can be anywhere between the Eastern and Full Eastern Backhand Grips.
(Please refer to the photo sequences on pages 32&33)

PREPARATION PHASE (PHOTOS 1&2)
Begins by a bending of the knees. There is a unit turn where the movement of the racket backwards occurs together with a shoulder rotation and a rear foot pivot. All three girls are well behind the handle on the grip with slight variations between Eastern and Full Eastern. Each player uses the non-dominant hand to help prepare the racket and to turn the upper body during the stroke. The body weight can be seen to be shifting from the back foot to the front foot as the girls step into their backhands. Note how they are very much looking over their right shoulders towards the oncoming ball as it approaches. See how the racket is taken high above the level of the back shoulder. All three girls have shoulders level and an excellent balance base.

FORWARD SWING TO CONTACT (PHOTOS 3&4)
As the front foot is planted the forward swing begins. The girls have stepped towards the ball and have adopted a closed to square stance. Hardenne (in all white) has closed more than the others with a larger step across. Immediately as the front foot is landed the racket head is dropped beneath the height of the ball. This now facilitates the movement of a low to high racket path and with the accompanying brushing up the back of the ball, plenty of topspin is generated. At contact the racket angle can be seen to be closed, the players heads stay still for a split second after. Contact occurs forward of the right shoulder and is relatively further forwards for the cross court compared to the down the line.

FOLLOW THROUGH (PHOTOS 5&6)
The shoulders and hips may finish 3/4 toward the net or fully open although this is largely a function of style and where the ball is being hit. Cross court shots will often lead to significant opening of the shoulders and hips. All three players demonstrate a beautiful high finish. The left leg moves forward to a position parallel with the right as the follow through comes to its completion to enable recovery.

JUSTINE-HENIN-HARDENNE

31

1   2   3

ALEXANDRA STEVENSON

1   2   3

JUSTINE HENIN-HARDENNE

1   2   3

AMELIE MAURESMO

4   5   6

4   5   6

4   5   6

THE TWO-HANDED TOPSPIN BACKHAND
THE GRIP
There are many variations used today. Typical variations include:

1. Two "slap on" Eastern Forehand grips.

2. One Continental with the right hand and one Eastern Forehand for the left.

3. One Continental with the right hand and one Semi Western with the left.

4. One Eastern Backhand with the right hand and one Semi Western or Western grip with the left.

On all of these grips both hands should be comfortably next to each other, not separated or overlapping. With today's high bouncing topspin oriented game it is recommended that players adopt either a Continental, Eastern or full Eastern Backhand grip for the right hand combined with a Semi Western Forehand grip for the left. The more extreme grip combinations keep the racket face closed throughout the backswing and forward swing. This keeps the racket face angle vertical to the ground, necessary for contact particularly at shoulder height.

(Please refer to the photo sequences on pages 35 and 36).

PREPARATION PHASE (PHOTOS 1 & 2)
Preparation commences with a bending of the knees. There is a unit turn where the movement of the racket backwards occurs together with a shoulder rotation and a rear foot pivot. Gambill takes the racket back low, Clijsters loops it and Kieffer takes it straight back. These differences are a function of style, not fundamentals.

PHOTO 2 demonstrates the beautiful early preparation being displayed. There is a full rotation of the shoulders with the rackets taken almost completely back well before the ball is upon them. The body weight has shifted to the back foot for all the players. Note how their shoulders are level and how they are looking over them at the oncoming ball.

FORWARD SWING TO CONTACT (PHOTOS 3&4)
Kieffer and Clijsters are really dropping the racket well beneath the ball just before the commencement of the forward swing. This indicates that they will be hitting with considerable topspin. Gambill hasn't dropped the wrists quite so much and will therefore hit with less topspin although his racket is still traveling on a low to high path. On contact the racket face angle of all three players is vertical to the ground and their left wrists are laid back, i.e. hyper-extended as a result of their grips. During contact as with the one handed topspin backhand the head remains stationary and the eyes focused on the contact region usually somewhat forward of the actual contact.

FOLLOW THROUGH (PHOTOS 5 & 6)
The follow throughs demonstrated by these photos are highly variable. The low to high trajectory developed immediately prior to contact continues in the early follow through. Both hands and the racket are generally positioned across or over the right shoulder at completion of the stroke.

 MARIA SHARAPOVA   VINCE SPADEA

34

1   2   3
JAN-MICHAEL GAMBILL

1   2   3
KIM CLIJSTERS

1   2   3
NICOLAS KIEFFER

INTRODUCTION TO SLICE

Backspin is generated when the underside of the ball rotates against air resistance. The ball is lifted and kept up longer by increased pressure below the ball. With side-spin whichever side of the ball rotates against air resistance will force the ball to swerve to the opposite side. In other words if you swing across the right side of the ball it will swerve to the left and vice versa. At an early stage in the development of the complete player the coach should introduce the student to slice. Always encourage a two handed player to develop a one handed sliced backhand hand in hand with the development of his two handed drive. This will give him added flexibility in terms of reach, handling high balls and playing approaches and drops. The Continental and Semi Continental grips provide the best feel for applying slice on the backhand side.

SLICED BACKHAND TEACHING PROGRESSIONS
1. LINE UP THE STUDENT
Move the student to a position just behind the service line, positioning him sideways to the net. Guide his racket into a position where the racket head is held above the back shoulder, the arm well bent and pulled close to the body **(fig 1).** The wrist should be cocked upwards or laid backwards. Ensure his left hand is supporting the racket at the throat by the finger tips.

2. SHADOW SWINGS
Demonstrate some shadow swings and have him follow. Check that his racket is swinging high to low, down through the desired point of contact with a good high finish. The racket face angle should correspond to the high to low racket path **(Figs 2,3,&4).** Make sure he finishes his swing with an open racket face **(fig 5).**

SLICED BACKHAND — fig 1, fig 2, fig 3, fig 4, fig 5

3. DROP FEEDING

Whilst ensuring his feet stay on the same spot proceed to drop feed him some balls. Encourage him to apply a downward glancing blow to the left and back of the ball, the wrist firm, his weight transferring forward into the shot. You will have to make frequent adjustments to the swing path and angle of his racket face before he starts to acquire the correct amounts of spin and speed to the ball.

4. SELF FEEDING

Now let him drop feed himself, directing him to take one step toward the ball before his forward swing. Direct him to adjust the height of each of his feeds, but making sure to hit all of them at the top of the bounce.

5. HAND FEEDING, RACKET FEEDING AND RALLYING

Proceed to go through the relevant feeding progressions until the student is capable of rallying sliced backhands baseline to baseline.

SLICED BACKHAND TECHNIQUE (Please refer to the photo sequences on pages 39 and 40)

PREPARATION PHASE (PHOTOS 1,2&3)

All three players have recognized that the ball is coming to their backhand side and have started the unit turn, i.e. the shoulders have turned at the same time as the rear foot pivot. Dent (top) is going to hit a backhand return and follow it in. Henin-Hardenne (middle) is hitting a neutralizing shot and Lapenti (bottom) is hitting a defensive shot to stay in the point. Both Henin-Hardenne and Dent use a one handed backhand, Lapenti a two-hander. Lapenti when utilizing the one handed slice slides his left hand up to the throat of the racket before finally releasing his left arm behind him. All three players have almost fully turned their shoulders. Note how they are looking over their shoulders at the oncoming ball. Note how:

A) The right arm is bent at the elbow and held close to the body.

B) The wrist is cocked upward or backward.

C) The racket head is held above the eventual point of ball contact.

FORWARD SWING TO CONTACT (PHOTO 4)

After the tremendous shoulder rotation, the players will now swing forward as they extend the elbow along with slight forearm rotation. All three players have started their swing forward and slightly onward to the ball. They start to extend their left hand backwards to aid in keeping their balance. Note the three different stances, Henin-Hardenne is hitting neutral, Dent closed and Lapenti open.

FOLLOW THROUGH (PHOTOS 5 & 6)

Note the full extension of the left arm as the players extend their follow through. This action also helps to generate more racket speed. The variation in their follow through reflects the different shots they are hitting. Dent is executing a down the line, inside out, return of serve approach shot. Henin-Hardenne is hitting a standard cross court shot. Lapenti is just trying to get the ball up over the net by opening the racket face.

1 2 3

TAYLOR DENT

1 2 3

JUSTINE HENIN-HARDENNE

1 2 3

NICHOLAS LAPENTI

SLICED FOREHAND

1. LINE UP THE STUDENT
Move the student to a position just behind the service line and position him in a sideways to the net forehand stance racket held high, wrist cocked upwards **(fig 1)**.

2. SHADOW SWINGS
Demonstrate some shadow swings and have him follow. Ensure that the racket is swinging high to low, down through the point of contact with a good high finish. The racket face angle should correspond to the high to low racket path **(Figs 2,3&4)**. Make any adjustments where necessary.

3. DROP FEEDING
Give him some feeds, ensuring both feet stay on the same spot. Encourage him to apply a downward glancing blow to the right and back of the ball, the wrist firm. Make sure that there is a smooth transfer of weight on to the front foot. Be prepared to make frequent adjustments to the path and angle of the racket face before he starts to acquire the correct amounts of speed and spin to the ball.

4. SELF FEEDING
Now let him drop feed himself directing him to take one step toward the ball before the forward swing. Direct him to adjust the height of each of his feeds and to take them at the top of the bounce. Work particularly hard on higher balls concentrating on bringing them down and making them land low.

5.HAND FEEDING, RACKET FEEDING AND RALLYING
Proceed to go through the relevant feeding progressions until the student is ready to rally sliced forehands baseline to baseline.

SLICED FOREHAND

fig 1

fig 2

fig 3

fig 4

fig 5

41

THE SERVICE

INTRODUCTION

When teaching anyone the serve from the youngest to the oldest, the least competent to the most capable always remember that some will possess more of a natural ability to throw a tennis racket with relatively good technique from the word go. Others will not and it is often because they don't have a good natural throwing action. When coaching groups of beginners you can normally tell who is going to have the best serve by requesting them to throw a few balls overarm at the beginning of the lesson.

Most will be able to shadow the service swing that you show them without the ball, however, when they try to co-ordinate the swing with the ball toss the strangest things will start to happen. Arms will stiffen and fail to bend, ball tosses will go everywhere, feet will move in all directions, elbows will drop completely. This is where a good instructor really comes into his own. It is crucial that the student be given the confidence enhancing means to get the ball over that net and into the service box very early with something that resembles a serve. From this point on the student can play and rally. This is where the following training method works so efficiently. It breaks down the serve and enables the students to familiarise themselves with the necessary movements on the serve, enabling the correct technique to be built into the muscle memory more quickly. This method reinforces quick learning and protects from regression, where a serve gets much worse rather than better. Use this method carefully to match the ability of each individual. Guide each student into serving with good balance, a steady toss, a good arm bend and relatively high elbow. This basic foundation will really put them on the right path.

INTRODUCING THE BASIC FLAT SERVICE

For the first lesson in serving line up the students and demonstrate some slow to medium paced flat serves. Emphasize a relaxed easy swing, the smoothness of the place up and its ideal height i.e. approximately 1ft higher than the outstretched racket arm. At this stage serve without moving the feet from the spot they are on. Show that they may rise up, but make it clear that by keeping them in the same place it will be easier to maintain balance and just as importantly control over the toss. This is the best method to ensure that a sound swing starts to shape up and that the automatic grooving process is initiated. Line up the students and set them up in the correct serving stance (**PHOTO 1**). Make sure that their feet are positioned so that a line drawn between the toes leads to the aim point, in this instance directly ahead. A racket placed on the ground can be used as a pointer for correct positioning of the feet (**PHOTO 2**). The feet should be about shoulder width apart.

PHOTO 1   PHOTO 2

THE GRIP

When training very young students like the children in **PHOTO 1** let them use an Eastern Forehand grip. For older and more skilled students attempt to introduce a modified Eastern Forehand or Continental grip. Some will feel uncomfortable with these grips but urge the students to adopt them clearly outlining the advantages and suitability for creating spin and speed on the ball. Show that in order to hit a flat serve when hitting with the modified Eastern and Continental grips the forearm and wrist must be pronated or turned from right to left. If the student only feels comfortable with an Eastern Forehand grip then let it be. The grip can be moved over at a later time when the student is more ready.

SERVICE TEACHING PROGRESSIONS

1. FROM SHOULDER TO CONTACT
With rackets rested on their back shoulders request the students to reach up and stretch their rackets to a contact position to the side and slightly in front of them. Have them repeat this at least five times. For those with a Semi-Continental or Continental grip the forearm and wrist must be turned or pronated from right to left to present the racket face vertical and flat on to the back of the ball.

2. THE FENCE TRAP
Move the students within about one foot of the back fence. With balls held at thigh level have the students toss their ball and trap it against the fence (**PHOTOS 3 & 4**). Repeat the exercise until each student traps at least one ball successfully.

3. CONTACT TAP FROM BACK SCRATCH POSITION
Move the students up to the service line, or halfway between the service line and the baseline (**PHOTO 5**). Now start with a deeper backswing, the rackets in a down the back or back scratch position. Ensure that all racket arm elbows are at least level or up and pointing to the back fence behind them. Have the students toss the ball and have them contact it at the point of contact and tap the ball forwards straight.

4. ADD FOLLOW THROUGH
Have them do the same and this time add a follow through, the racket finishing nicely past the left side.

5. MINI-SERVICE CONTEST
Now would be a good time to introduce a mini-service competition. Move the students to just behind the service line. Introduce mini-serves with each server serving straight to the box in front. Encourage the servers to hit up on the ball and check that their follow throughs are working correctly.

6. COORDINATION OF THE PLACE UP AND SWING

Here the students must learn to place the ball up and take their rackets into the back scratch position at the same time. Encourage them to think of together-one-two in their minds, with arms going down together on one and then releasing the ball with a straight arm on two, racket dropped nicely down to finish.

The ball should be caught in the place up hand as an addition to this exercise. Make sure to stagger this practice, i.e. 15 seconds 1-2 without the ball and 15 seconds with it. The movement will come together very quickly in this way. In the early stages of learning the serve make sure to keep the student's bodies relatively straight with only a very limited back arch and knee bend. These can be built into the service action at a later stage. For now, good balance and a consistent place up are the chief concerns. Make sure to emphasize the importance of keeping the feet on the same spot during this exercise. They may raise up, but must stay in the same position.

As the level of competency increases encourage the students to actually hit some balls instead of catching them. If the students feel more comfortable touching their backs with their rackets this is fine because it gives them instant information as to where the racket is behind them and helps to preserve a good backswing. Encourage the more skilled students to practice the above exercise, pausing the racket in the position shown in **PHOTO 6**. They must catch the ball with the racket held in this position. When they try hitting from this position make sure that the backswing stays sound.

Next the students must learn to coordinate the place up with the full swing. Here a good aid is to have the students think of a "1-2-3" number sequence on the serve. Starting on one, the arms go down together, the ball is released on two. The one-two needs to be quick, the hit coming on three, just a little later. Encourage the students to shadow swing with these numbers in their minds, synchronizing the method with the numbers. For the students learning to pause in the trophy position shown in **PHOTO 6** below the rhythm should be established a little differently with a 1-2 hold 3-4 effect.

PHOTO 6

44

SERVICE IN MOTION
Let us now take a look at the complete service motion in action.

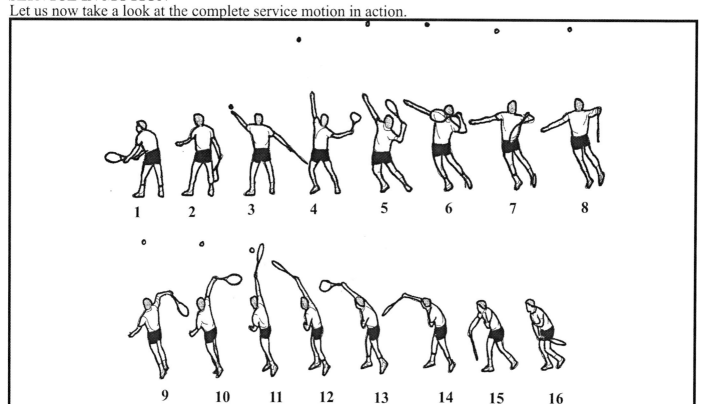

1. The racket arm and place up arm are very much together at the start. Body weight may be evenly distributed, on the front foot or the back foot.

2&3. The racket is swung pendulum like in a low downward and upward arc. The body weight shifts to the back foot. The arms part around thigh level, the left arm straightens and the wrist also stays straight.

3&4. The upper body turns away from the net toward the side fencing on the right. The racket arm continues to rise up and the knees start to bend. The ball is released around forehead level or above as body weight shifts on to the front foot.

5. The racket rises up into the classic trophy position pointing toward the sky, the left arm is fully extended. At this point the racket may pause before the throw or it can move on continuously. The knees should be bent to their fullest and the back arched. From this position the legs thrust up and forwards to the ball.

6&7. Going up to the contact point, the body straightens, the knees being the first to straighten. The elbow continues to bend as the racket drops down the back.

8. The racket is at its lowest point behind the back, the knees are completely straight.

9&10. The racket accelerates up to the contact point and the wrist comes into play. The pronation of the arm just before the contact turns the racket face at a right angle to the direction of the shot. To pronate the racket correctly the forearm and wrist must be turned from right to left and outward.

11. At contact the shoulder of the striking arm is as high as possible, the racket arm completely straight. The racket head is practically vertical to the ground. The left hand is held in front of the body for stability.

12,13 & 14. The upper body follows the ball in the direction of the stroke.

15&16. The right arm swings in front of the body and to the left side. The left arm remains in front of the body. The right foot comes through fully and supports the body weight as it lands on the ground. With this serve the left foot stays anchored (although raised up) maintaining balance throughout the action.

VARIATIONS ON THE SERVE

1. Ball toss and backswing
A) Both arms can be lowered and raised simultaneously.
B) The upward movement of the ball hand can be relatively quick and short.
C) The racket arm can be moved downward and the ball arm raised. Depending on how the various individual movements are strung together, they effect how high the ball is tossed. Many players such as Andy Roddick prefer a short backswing, using no pendulum movement, this helps with coordination and timing.

2. Footwork variations
A) The back foot will be moved up or dragged into a position behind the front foot. This will occur as the knees are fully bent just before the feet leave the ground. The left foot will land first before the right foot steps ahead just afterwards. This is the more commonly used footwork.
B) The back foot will step into the court as the racket comes through to contact, **(see service in motion page 45).** The front foot will stay in contact with the ground but will raise up. Sometimes both feet will leave the ground during this motion.
C) Both feet will stay in place and will leave the ground as the knees are fully bent just before the explosion into the serve. The left foot will land first and the right foot will step just after.

3. Turning of the racket hand inward at the start
At the start of the backswing the hand is turned inward toward the court. This helps to ensure that the wrist at the top of the action with the racket pointing upwards fails to fall away to the right. This should guarantee a solid throwing action.

SERVICE FAULTS AND CURES
FAULT 1 The elbow fails to bend, causing failure of the racket to drop behind the back.

CURE 1 Encourage the student to touch the back very lightly with the racket, keeping the arm as relaxed as possible during the swing.

CURE 2 Shadow the action with a two finger grip and then try to do the same while hitting.

CURE 3 Start the action repeatedly from a backscratch position with the racket tucked inside the right shoulder blade and almost touching the small of the back.

FAULT 2 The wrist flicks the ball away at the end of the toss.

CURE Ensure the ball is held between the first two fingers and the thumb. Guide the student into rolling the ball off and away, (use the analogy of releasing a bird from the hand).

FAULT 3 The place up is always wayward.

CURE 1 Ensure that the feet stay on the same spot during the action, making sure not to chase errant tosses.

CURE 2 Practice placing the ball up and catching it in the desired spot.

CURE 3 Repeat the fence trap drill.

FAULT 4 The place up is always too low.

CURE 1 Toss the ball up for the student.

CURE 2 Concentrate exclusively on the continuity of the swing and work the place up into this rather than trying to make the swing fit the place up.

FAULT 5 Quick tossing arm.

CURE Encourage the student to keep the tossing arm up for a count of two before dropping it.

FAULT 6 Body off balance.

CURE 1 Ensure that the feet stay on the same spot during the action and that there is a good weight transfer back foot to front foot.

CURE 2 Ensure that in the early days of developing the serve the body stays reasonably straight, with no premature knee bends. Arching of the back and a proper knee bend can be built into the serve at a later stage.

FAULT 7 The racket is drawn back too close to the side.

CURE Ensure that the racket is allowed to flow freely to the side of the student.

FAULT 8 Swing too jerky or discontinuous.

CURE Serve with the side of the racket, switching to the full face at the last second.

ROGER FEDERER

PHOTO 7

FAULT 9 Racket uncontrolled or wavering through the backswing.

CURE   Make sure the racket is supported along the handle with all the fingers making sure none are released prematurely.

FAULT 10 The elbow relaxes and drops too low as the racket comes up.

CURE 1   Practice repeated swings with the elbow pointing upwards from a deep down the back position.

CURE 2   Make sure to touch the back during the action and at the same time push up the elbow before throwing the racket at the ball.

CURE 3   Bounce the tossed ball on your raised elbow.

ADVANCED SERVING

1. THE FLAT SERVICE

This type of service can be hit with the Eastern Forehand, Semi-Continental and Continental grips. It is hit with an upward hitting motion common to all serves which naturally places a slight degree of topspin to the ball. It is a very useful serve for a fast court such as grass or fast hard where the speed of the court will give a very good chance of many service winners and aces.

The ball moving from the racket face to the service court will travel on a very low trajectory with little spin and therefore very limited margin for error. Therefore to make this service really consistent and accurate you must go out and practice it regularly. To make it effective you should be able to hit it 70% plus into court in a match situation. To achieve this you should develop a 3/4 pace version that you can hit deep to the receiver's backhand, forehand, or into his body at will. Because of the very direct path of this serve it is easy for the receiver to read and so you must keep good speed on the ball to keep him rushed and bothered. If he starts to lock on to it you should start varying it with topspin and sliced deliveries to throw him off his rhythm.

Today this serve is less commonly hit than the flat with topspin where the server comes across the right hand corner of the ball rather than just directly up and through it. Here the ball travels with slightly more of an arc on its trajectory and more controlling spin, therefore allowing for more margin for error.

2. THE SLICED SERVE

The ball should be placed a little more to the right on a line level with the hitting shoulder. It can be used as a first serve and many great servers have used it to great effect at Wimbledon including John McKenroe, Martina Navratilova and Kevin Curren. All the above players were left handers and could take the receiver right out into the add court on the backhand side and then play the first volley into the open court. For a right hander the effect of the racket strings cutting across the outside right of the ball from right to left will cause the ball to swerve from right to left. It is particularly useful for swerving into the body of an accomplished returner.

3. THE TOPSPIN SERVICE

This is the most widely used second serve mainly as a result of its high security factor. Like topspin ground strokes you can hit it high over the net with the knowledge that the resulting bound forwards will provide protection from attack. This serve demands more of an exaggerated shoulder turn, back arch and knee bend than the basic service, and the up and across direction of the edge on racket is also different. The ball is placed more over to the left, the racket strings brushing up or deflecting the ball rather than directly hitting it. By varying the amount of speed and spin this serve can be used as an effective first serve because it provides consistency and more time for the incoming serve and volleyer to get in behind it.

4. THE KICK SERVE

This is the close relative of the topspin service. The ball is struck much more left to right across the back of the ball. This gives the effect of kicking the ball out to the receiver's left on the bounce. If you can get enough height and movement on the kick you will have the means to take the receiver right out of court on his backhand side in the add court.

GORAN IVANISEVIC

PHOTO 8

Make sure to develop more than just one spin serve.
Give yourself as many options as possible and you will be
far more ready out on that match court.

THE GRIP
Use a Continental or Eastern Backhand grip for spin serving.
This will help to give you the necessary angle of racket face
and flexibility for fast wrist movement.

SLICE
Try to imagine the back of the tennis ball as a clock face
(Opposite). When hitting slice hit the ball at the two or three
O'clock position. The ball should be placed to the right,
in line with the hitting shoulder **(PHOTO 9).**

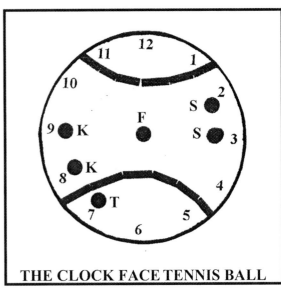

THE CLOCK FACE TENNIS BALL

TOPSPIN
Topspin serves are played diagonally across from 7 at the bottom
to 1 or 2 at the top. The ball should be placed far more to the left, more
in line with the head and slightly more behind compared to a toss for a flat or slice **(PHOTO 10).**

KICK
The kick serve is played with a more exaggerated left to right movement from 8 or 9 to 2 o'clock.

Please note the position of the ball toss in the photos below.

**PHOTO 9
SLICED SERVE**

**PHOTO 10
TOPSPIN SERVE**

THE MODERN SERVICE

Please look at the serving sequence shots of Pete Sampras, Roger federer and Justine Henin-Hardenne taken from front, side and back respectively on the next two pages. Note the tremendous technique used by all three as they launch themselves up and into their motions.

PHOTO 1
Note how all three players have transferred their body weight to the back foot and turned their shoulders away from the net ensuring their tossing arms stay well clear and to the right side of their bodies.

PHOTO 2
Note the tremendous bend of the knees and the classic trophy position racket, held pointing upward to the sky. Power comes from the ground up and all three players can be seen to be driving up and through the ball as a consequence of the push from this knee position. All three players use a back foot back style which results in a more linear or forward movement into the serve. Other players such as Carlos Moya and Ivan Lubicic use a back foot up to the front style before pushing off which results in a more upward movement.

PHOTO 3
See the racket position of all three players, i.e. fully extended down the back. The knees are now completely straight.

PHOTO 4
All three players can be seen to be contacting the ball well out in front. The ideal ball position for top servers such as these is around 8 inches to the left of the front foot. From this contact position players such as Federer and Sampras can better disguise their serve. It becomes extremely difficult for their opponents to know whether they are about to receive a flat, kick or sliced delivery.

PHOTO 5
After contact all three player's forearms continue to pronate outwards to the right.

PHOTO 6
Racket deceleration and recovery are clearly seen in the final shots. All players exhibit great balance. The landing pattern will often be dependent on the game style or the tactics of the player at that particular moment. Sampras is aiming on moving forwards and serve and volleying. Hardenne is looking to recover quickly to the baseline. Federer is landing in a position where he can elect to either move forward or stay back.

1   2   3

PETE SAMPRAS

1   2   3

JUSTINE HENIN-HARDENNE

1   2   3

ROGER FEDERER

THE FOREHAND VOLLEY

Demonstrate the motion of a forehand volley emphazising the brief compact blocking movement of the racket. Explain that when volleying fast balls close to the net, backswing is limited solely to the amount of shoulder turn allowed. Make it clear that when standing back or hitting a softer approaching ball it is sometimes necessary to increase the amount of backswing and follow through slightly. Move on to teaching the basic shoulder high volley using the following steps. We will relate to the individual situation.

PHOTO 1

PHOTO 2

1. LINING UP THE STUDENT

Line up your student in a forehand sideways standing position to the net, outstretched racket length away in an Eastern Forehand grip. The racket should be held well in front, the arm bent at the elbow, the wrist cocked **(PHOTO 1)**

PHOTO 3

PHOTO 4

2. SIMPLE FEEDING

Feed simple feeds with targets such as cones, racket covers or chairs (between the legs) placed in front so the student can concentrate on moving his racket forwards and deflecting the ball downward into the court. Progress to giving some feeds which allow the student to take a step forwards to the ball **(PHOTO 2)**.

3. TURNING, STEPPING AND HITTING FROM FORWARDS FACING READY POSITION

With the technique beginning to take shape move him into a forwards facing ready position making sure he stays alert and springy **(PHOTO 3)**. Now give feeds which allow time for him to turn and step at the same time into the path of the oncoming ball. Encourage him to make contact as early as possible, at the same time as his front foot touches the ground **(PHOTO 4)**.

COMMON FAULTS AND CURES ON THE VOLLEY

FAULT 1 Racket unstable or floppy wrist on contact.
CURE 1 Firm up the wrist by lightly squeezing the racket handle on contact.
CURE 2 Hold the racket higher up the handle and do the same as above.

FAULT 2 Inability to coordinate the step and hit together.
CURE Repeatedly shadow the stroke and the correct footwork together with a quick one two guide.

FAULT 3 Too much backswing.
CURE Set up the student in a position right up against the back fencing so so that the racket will immediately touch the fence when taken back.

FAULT 4 Too much follow through.
CURE 1 Encourage the hitter to imagine an edgeways facing mirror extending from his middle. If the racket crosses this line the glass is broken.
CURE 2 Practice plenty of volleying right up close to the practice wall.

PHOTO 5

BACKHAND VOLLEY

Demonstrate the motion of both the basic one-handed and two-handed backhand volleys. If the student is very young or weaker wristed then introduce a two hander.

ONE-HANDED

1. LINING UP THE STUDENT

Position the student in a backhand sideways standing position with an Eastern Backhand or Continental grip, racket in the desired position. The racket should be held well out in front of the body, the arm slightly bent, the wrist cocked. The racket face should be supported by the fingers of the non-playing hand **(PHOTO 5)**.

2. SIMPLE FEEDING

Again give some feeds with targets placed in front, with the purpose of developing a downwards deflecting feel into the court. Give some feeds which allow the student to make a quick forwards step **(PHOTO 6)**.

3. TURNING, STEPPING AND HITTING FROM FORWARDS FACING READY POSITION

Move the student into a forwards facing ready position and give feeds which give him time to turn, step and make the contact at the correct instant **(PHOTO 7)**. Make sure the arm is straight on contact, the wrist firm.

PHOTO 6

PHOTO 7

55

TWO-HANDED BACKHAND VOLLEY

Give the student a Continental or Sem-Continental grip for the bottom hand and an Eastern Forehand grip for the top.

1. LINING UP THE STUDENT
Again position him in a sideways standing position, the racket held out in front, both hands placed comfortably along the handle **(PHOTO 8)**.

2. SIMPLE FEEDING
Direct your feeds to his racket requesting him to edge both wrists forward, pushing the left or top wrist more dominantly on the contact. Again give some feeds which allow for a quick forward step **(PHOTO 9)**.

3.TURNING STEPPING AND HITTING FROM FORWARDS FACING READY POSITION
As with the forehand and one-handed backhand volleys, starting from forwards, direct him to turn, step and make the contact with the quick 1-2 pattern **(PHOTO 10)**.

FAULTS
Common to the forehand volley are common to the backhand and their cures may be applied the same.

ALTERNATE VOLLEYING
When the student becomes more competent with his volleys start feeding him alternate volleys, forehand and backhand.

VOLLEY-VOLLEY
1. Standing on opposite sides of the net, practice volley volley to each other's forehand.
2. Make sure to line up your rackets opposite each other and to concentrate on lofting the ball upwards. This will give your student more time and help to maintain longer rallies.
3. Always start each rally with a volley feed. As the level of competency increases move back, lower the ball and rally cross court.
4. Now do the same on the backhand.
5. Introduce alternate volley-volley with one player going cross, the other straight.

PHOTO 8

PHOTO 9

PHOTO 10

ADVANCED VOLLEYING

In the preceding section on the volley we looked at how the basic forehand and backhand volley are introduced to the student. Here the student learns to place the racket at the intended point of contact and move it forward to intercept the ball with a blocking motion. The grip is changed from Eastern Forehand to Eastern Backhand or Continental depending on what is required. These grips give good support in the early stages of volleying. Moving from beginner, through intermediate and advanced, volleying becomes much more significant in your game and various volleying techniques will have to be learnt to make you a more complete player. Most importantly the increase in the speed of the tennis will mean that it is recommended to volley with one grip on both forehand and backhand. Here a Continental or Semi-Continental grip will give you the necessary flexibility, particularly when handling fast volley exchanges. Smashes and half volleys should also be learnt with these grips.

THE BASIC SHOULDER HIGH VOLLEY

This volley should be played with a touch of backspin on both forehand and backhand so as to give you that necessary ball control. The ball is struck with a downward glancing blow with the racket face slightly opened. This will help to keep the ball low when it bounces.

THE LOW VOLLEY

When the ball gets between you and the net, get down with your knees and make sure to keep the racket head up. Step with the front foot before the contact. Open your racket face with your forearm and wrist with enough angle to clear the net and hit deep into your opponent's court.

THE DROP VOLLEY

The drop volley is a soft touch shot meant to drop the ball vertically over the other side of the net before fading. It is normally played off slower drives than its close relative, the stop volley. It is often a good tactic to use this shot as a surprise variation, particularly against a slow footed opponent. Play it by loosening your grip at impact, let your racket recoil slightly as the ball hits and at the same time turn your wrist and forearm quickly in a clockwise direction (on a forehand) to put backspin on the ball.

THE STOP VOLLEY

The stop volley is played off much faster drives and like the drop volley can be used as a surprise to the normal angled or deep volley. This shot requires excellent timing and is technically similar to the drop volley in that the grip is relaxed on contact, although the ball should die much more suddenly on the other side of the net.

HIGH VOLLEY

On the high forehand and backhand volleys make sure to keep the wrist or wrists (two handed) firm, all the way through the backswing, contact and follow through. Keep them turned inward toward the court to make sure the ball doesn't fly.

FOREHAND DROP VOLLEY

BACKHAND DROP VOLLEY

THE DRIVE VOLLEY

When you want to hit really aggressively on the volley, particularly on soft high floating balls, the drive volley is the answer. Here you can swing fully at the stroke, generating racket head speed either by arm action alone (at the shoulder) or by combining arm action with shoulder rotation. This shot can be played in two different ways:

1. With a firm wrist where the result will be a kind of one-piece swing with no slack at the wrist or elbow **(see figs 1-8 below).**

2. With a loose wrist and elbow where a fast arm action will help to create terrific topspin. Andre Agassi is particularly known for his topspin drive volleys off both sides.

DRIVE VOLLEY

THE LOB VOLLEY

Here the grip is relaxed and the racket face opened sharply to allow the ball to be played over the head of the net man. It is a particularly useful shot in doubles when four players are facing each other at the net. Play the shot with a shortened follow through. This shot requires a very fine touch **(see forehand and backhand figs 1-5).**

FOREHAND LOB VOLLEY

BACKHAND LOB VOLLEY

THE RETURN OF SERVE

The service is the single most important stroke in tennis, but you will find it very difficult to move up high on the tennis ladder without a good return of service. All the greats of tennis have or have had great returns, including Jimmy Connors and Andre Agassi. Over the years both players have displayed the best returning seen on a tennis court. The secret of great returning lies in the ability to see the ball fast and react fast. Always be alert, stay on the balls of your feet, stand in. As your opponent tosses up the ball move forwards and just before he makes his contact make sure to split step. This will ensure that you are ready to react very quickly and stay aggressive on the return. By using this technique you can lock in to the rhythm of your opponent and most importantly synchronize your timing on the return with his timing on the serve. Try to focus on the following footwork and positioning habits, you will definitely be returning better if you apply these techniques.

1. THE FAST FIRST SERVE

Here make the split step and move into the serve with one step forwards, similar to that on the volley, together with the contact. On the backhand, lead with your right foot. Lead with your left foot on the forehand. Some serves will come in so fast there's no time to take this step. Here make a very quick shoulder turn, stand your ground, and block the ball back. You can play open stance forehand and backhand on such returns.
When you feel you are picking up the speed of these serves get out of the "blocking mode" and get into the "playing it back with interest mode" whereby you add a restricted backswing that really utilizes your opponent's pace. This is where you can start to regain the initiative and use the opponent's pace against him. If the serve is moving away from you try to move sideways and diagonally forwards at the same time **(See fig 1, page 61 for receiver's best positioning for returning a hard, deep serve).**

2. 3/4 AND MEDIUM PACED SERVES

Again, you must move forwards, split step and try to get the front foot down before the contact, more like a conventional ground stroke step before driving the return **(fig 2, page 61).**

3. SLOW AND SECOND SERVES

For the slower or short second serves, move directly ahead to the ball, split step and take it is as early as you can. Either drive with topspin or chip with backspin. Some players particularly on slow red clay courts might elect to back up behind the baseline and take topspin second serves on the fall. Thomas Muster, the great Austrian clay court specialist often used this technique. Returning on the second serve definitely involves more elements of strategy compared to the reactionary mode of first serve returning **(See fig 3, page 61).**

   ANDRE AGASSI   TIM HENMAN

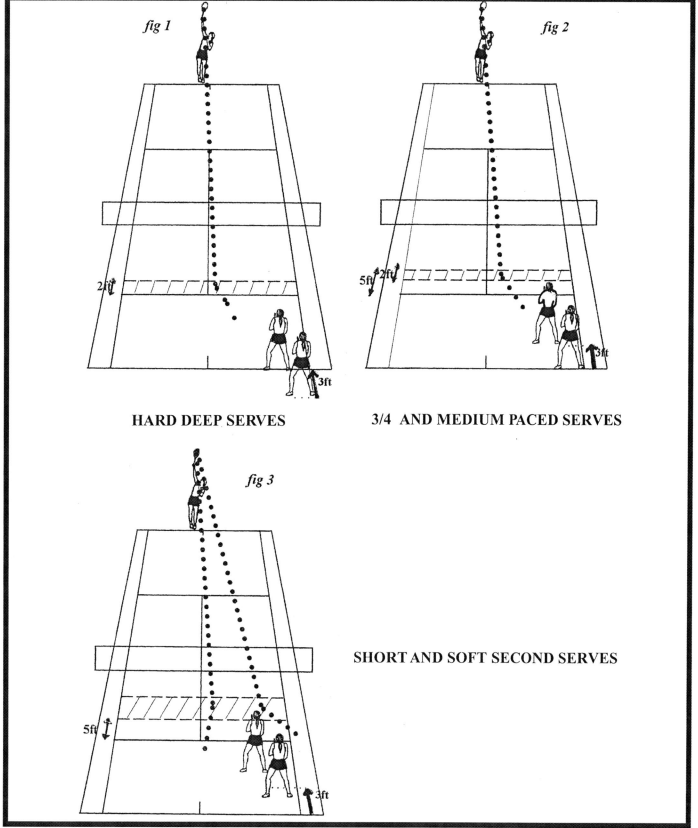

fig 1

HARD DEEP SERVES

fig 2

3/4 AND MEDIUM PACED SERVES

fig 3

SHORT AND SOFT SECOND SERVES

RETURN OF SERVE PRACTICE METHODS

1. Have your practice partner serve hard, deep serves first to the forehand and then to the backhand. If he doesn't trouble you enough with his speed ask him to move forward and serve from halfway between the service line and baseline. Practice a quick step forwards into the serve on both sides. Have him hit more to the sides and practice moving diagonally forwards to the ball. Also work on serves right into the body where you have to take some very quick adjustment steps away from the ball.

2. Have your partner serve 3/4 or medium paced serves where you have time to hit a more conventional topspin drive with the lead foot well planted on the ground before the hit.

3. Practice backspin chipped returns off topspin and kick serves coming in high to the forehand and backhand **(PHOTOS 1 & 2)**. Make sure also to work hard on driving with topspin on such balls, concentrating on keeping the racket face closed to keep the ball in the court.

QUICK TIPS: Keep your eye on the ball, not the server. His place up will often give clues as to what will happen next. If you have a grip that has to be changed for forehands and backhands, experiment on your receiving grip to see which one you can change the fastest.

PHOTO 1

PHOTO 2

TACTICAL CONSIDERATIONS

When practicing your returns gear your practice to simulating situations in singles and doubles separately.

SINGLES

1. Beginners should first practice returning deep down the middle off both forehand and backhand. From that point on in a match they can start trying to out-rally the opposition.

2. Intermediate and advanced players should practice targeting low up the center to simulate being attacked by an incoming serve and volleyer. Also hard and deep into the corners so as to rush or take out the baseliner.

DOUBLES

1. In doubles beginners should concentrate on returning cross court and use a lifted lob over the net man.

2. Intermediate and advanced doubles players must develop a sharply angled cross court return as well as the ability to hit hard and low cross court.

THE APPROACH SHOT

STROKE TECHNIQUE

1. Learn to play your approach shots on the move, making sure to steady yourself before the contact.

2. When approaching very short balls make sure to get to the ball as fast as you can. Play the ball at the top of the bounce, or even earlier on the rise. This will help to rush your opponent.

3. When hitting your backhand sliced approach, just before the contact draw the back foot up to the front foot or cross it over and bring it in front on the inside, both techniques are acceptable. This is a particularly useful technique when attacking a short second serve.

4. When attacking a short and low ball with a lifted topspin drive move to the ball as you would a normal ground stroke and move quickly. As you approach the ball make sure to turn sideways into a more neutral stance for the contact. This will help you to direct the approach much better and put more into it. For a higher ball and when you have more time turn sideways and side shuffle up to the ball before you play the approach.

PRACTICE METHODS

1. Start three ball rallies with your practice partner with you approaching on the third ball of each. Have him vary the depth of each set up ball and practice approaching from different parts of the court.

2. Practice sliced and topspin approaches down the lines and down the center of the court.

3. Practice varying the depth of your approaches, learning to dig the ball in around the service line with backspin, slicing curve balls 5 or 6 feet behind the service line and hitting topspin drives hard and deep down the middle and into the corners.

4. Have your partner serve second serves and practice moving forwards chipping down the line. Again vary the depth of your approaches off a variety of different positioned serves.

5. Practice the above, this time with topspin fast attacking drives.

TACTICAL CONSIDERATIONS

1. The approach shot is the vital link between defense and attack. Your net game will only ever be as good as your approach shot making ability.

2. The most basic tactic when approaching balls on the left and right hand sides of the court is to hit straight down that side, camp at the net that side of center and play your volley to the other side **(see approach shot figs 1&2 next page)**. Here the down the line pass is covered while your opponent's cross court pass is much more difficult. Always remember that it takes less time to move into a good net position when hitting down the line compared to cross court.

3. When approaching a ball positioned in the center of the court, a hard down-the-middle approach is a good option using a central net position to counter any passing shots either side **(See approach shot fig 3 next page)**.

4. Play cross court only to a pronounced weakness or to keep an opponent guessing.

5. Be careful in thinking only to hit deep on your approaches. You must hit deep at the correct times. Hitting deep tends to rule out the angles and you are often playing it right back to your opponent positioned behind the baseline. You are opening yourself up to the lob.

6. Good players learn to play their approaches with both subtlety and raw power. Develop your sliced approaches hand in hand with your forcing topspin approaches.

7. Good anticipation of the short ball helps to make the approach shot easier. Learn to feel when the shot may be short, e.g. resulting from your deep or hard shot, or perhaps because the opponent is off balance or had to run a great distance. Move forwards ready to attack the ball early and move in.

8. Follow the ball to the net. If your opponent is returning from a long way behind the baseline it's very likely he will lob, so don't get so close. Split to a balanced stop just before your opponent makes his contact, move to the ball and volley into the open court.

THE APPROACH SHOT

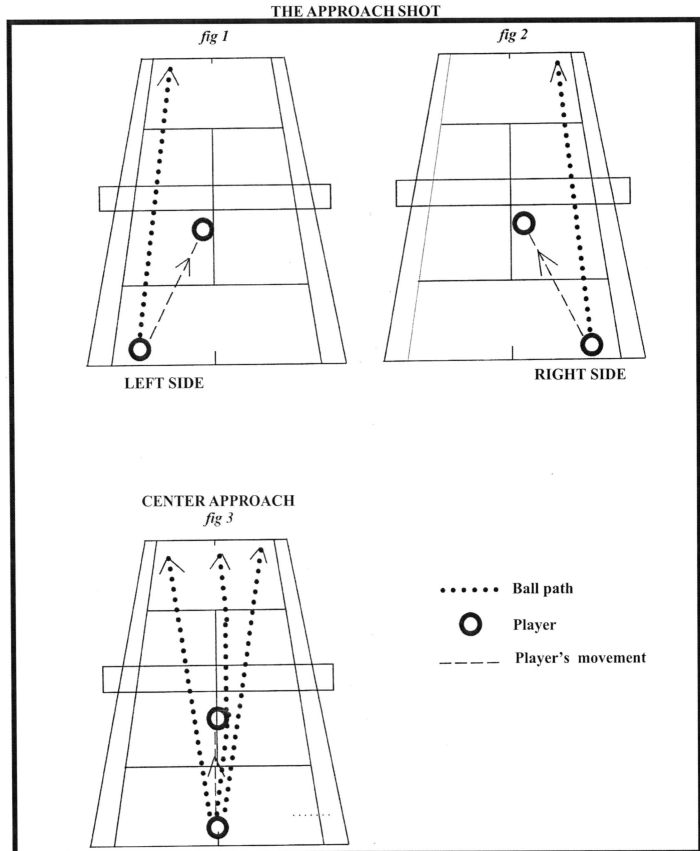

fig 1

LEFT SIDE

fig 2

RIGHT SIDE

CENTER APPROACH
fig 3

• • • • • • Ball path

O Player

– – – – Player's movement

SPECIALITY SHOTS

Always remember that if you don't have a practice partner or ball machine available you can practice many of the shots already mentioned and included in the following section against the practice wall or backboard. These include your groundstrokes including topspin and slice, volleys, half volleys, drop shots, serves and even overheads. The greatest players have all practiced hard against the practice wall which really helps to reinforce stroke technique and improve footwork, reactions, rhythm and timing.

THE DEFENSIVE LOB

The defensive lob should be introduced to beginners in the earliest stages. It helps to ingrain control of the racket face and feel into the system. Beginners and Intermediates will win more matches when they know how and when to use it.

STROKE TECHNIQUE

A) The preparation is the same as for the basic lifted drive, except that before the contact the racket head is lowered beneath the ball and the racket face opened **(figs 1,2,3,4 forehand and backhand next page)**.
B) The wrist should stay firm, and the body weight should transfer forward into the shot.
C) The follow through should finish with the racket hand finishing well above head height at the end of the swing. Height will be lost if you pull away too soon on the follow through **(figs ,5,6 forehand and backhand next page and photos 1&2 below)**.

PRACTICE METHODS

A) Practice self feeding from both a closed and neutral stance.
B) Place a row of tennis balls halfway between the service line and the base line and concentrate on making every lob carry past this line. Avoid going short. Always go for depth even if it means deliberately playing some long.
C) Imagine a wall placed 15 feet above the net in front of you. Make sure to practice self feeding from different points on, inside and behind the baseline and clear the wall. Place another set of balls three feet inside the baseline to further test your accuracy.
D) Work with your hitting partner on the ball machine and start with simple feeding, then build it up and make it wider and faster.
E) Force yourself to play lobs from a more open stance position where you would abbreviate the backswing and add more backspin to keep control of the ball.
F) Practice the same methods on the backhand side. Ensure that if you are double-handed you learn a good defensive lob with one hand. This will give you extra reach and the ability to get to the widest of balls.

FOREHAND DEFENSIVE LOB

BACKHAND DEFENSIVE LOB

PHOTO 1

PHOTO 2

65

FOREHAND DEFENSIVE LOB

BACKHAND DEFENSIVE LOB

3. TACTICAL CONSIDERATIONS

A) This shot is normally played when your opponent gets aggressive and attacks the net. Here by lobbing over the net man, followed by your own fast net advance, defense can quickly be turned into attack.

B) Good lobs can buy recovery time, meaning added time to recover court position quickly.

C) When rallying, the lob is a very useful change of pace shot, good for upsetting the rhythm of your opponent.

D) When under more pressure, i.e. with faster and wider balls, generally limit backswing and add more height and backspin to the ball.

THE TOPSPIN LOB

The topspin lob off both forehand and backhand is an essential part of the complete player's arsenal. With good passing shots and topspin lobs you will always be able to keep the net rusher guessing.

STROKE TECHNIQUE

A) The preparation starts the same as for the basic lifted drive, but the racket head should be dropped very low at the end of the backswing **(figs 1,2,3 forehand and backhand below).**
B) From here a very fast wrist action brushing up the back of the ball will give a great deal of topspin.
C) The follow through should finish higher than the basic lifted drive, **(figs 4,5,6 forehand and backhand below).**

PRACTICE METHODS

A) Practice self feeding from both an open and neutral stance. Make sure to give yourself plenty of height on the bounce to give time to enable you to drop the racket head very low under the ball.
B) Practice with your partner hitting approach shots, yourself responding with forehand and backhand topspin lobs from all over the court.
C) Make sure to test your accuracy by using the line markers as mentioned before (in the defensive lob section).

TACTICAL CONSIDERATIONS

A) The topspin lob is the ultimate counter punching shot against an aggressive volleyer. When played well and with disguise it will likely force a mistake from your opponent or enable you to make an outright winner.
B) The lower trajectory and faster speed of this shot makes timing on the smash particularly more difficult. Generally give yourself more court to hit into by going cross court with the topspin lob particularly when running wide and with good time to make the shot.

FOREHAND TOPSPIN LOB

BACKHAND TOPSPIN LOB

THE HALF VOLLEY

The half volley is essentially a pick up stroke where the ball is played on the short hop. You are often forced to play half volleys on your way into the net or when defending from the baseline.

STROKE TECHNIQUE (Refer to forehand and backhand figures below).

1. Use a very short backswing.
2. The racket face should be more opened the closer you get to the net. Here minor adjustments have to be made with the wrist and forearm.
3. Keep the wrist firm and the edge of the racket face very close to the ground.
4. Get down to the ball with a very good knee bend making sure to keep the head still when playing the shot.
5. Go to the ball and make contact well in front of the body.
6. Adjust the length of the stroke, depending on your distance from the net and your aim point.

PRACTICE METHODS

1. Practice with your hitting partner playing repeated half volleys service line to service line.
2. Start on the baseline and move to the net at the same time, playing half volleys until you arrive there.
3. Play repeated half volleys against the practice wall.

TACTICAL CONSIDERATIONS

1. When played from mid-court the shot maintains the forward movement to the net against the low return.
2. When defending on the baseline it helps maintain a good position on the court.
3. It helps recovery in difficult situations.

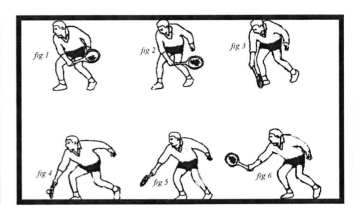

FOREHAND HALF VOLLEY   **BACKHAND HALF VOLLEY**

THE DROP SHOT

Just like the defensive lob the drop shot should be introduced in the earliest stages, helping the student to learn control of the racket face and feel. Intermediate and advanced players must learn to use the shot as a surprise element and so the art of disguise should be built in when practicing it.

TECHNIQUE

A) Prepare for the stroke as you would a basic sliced forehand or backhand drive. **(See fig 1,2&3 below).**
B) Come down and take the pace off the ball with a slow forward swing, the racket face angle approximately 45 degrees. The resulting backspin should hold down the bounce as the ball lands **(See fig 4 forehand and backhand below).**
C) Use a very abbreviated follow through.**(see fig 5 forehand and backhand below).**

PRACTICE METHODS

A) Start playing drop shots with your hitting partner, alternating forehands and backhands from the service lines, and work your way forwards.
B) Play 11 ups (11 point games) inside the service boxes playing drop shots only. You will have to work good angles to get mistakes out of your partner. This is good for getting the feel of the shot.
C) Rally with your partner baseline to baseline, one nominated to drop shot the other. Drop at least one time after your first drive within the next four, making a big effort to disguise the shot successfully. Score points for each successful drop shot.
D) Learn to play your drop shots off drives which naturally have a high backswing such as the sliced forehand and backhand and looped forehand. Your success in disguising the shot will be much higher when shaping up to hit these shots.

TACTICAL CONSIDERATIONS

A) Use plenty of drop shots against a baseliner who never comes to the net. Force him to play some volleys and overheads, shots that he might not be able to hit at all.
B) Always be able to play the shot with at least some disguise and never from behind the baseline.
C) Play it mostly straight, but learn the ability to angle it also.
D) It is a very effective shot against a slow-footed opponent, but also effective when the opponent is off balance or out of position.

FOREHAND DROP SHOT

BACKHAND DROP SHOT

69

THE SMASH

The smash is the basic counter to the lob, similar to the service in form, but played with an abbreviated backswing. The secret to a good smash is a quick turn, quick feet and good timing. Just like the flat serve the ball is struck at its back in an up and through motion. This will give the fastest speed on the ball, although there will be occasional times when some controlling spin is required. Play the stroke with your serving grip.

TECHNIQUE

1. From the volley ready position step back with your right foot as soon as you see the lob from your opponent **(see figs 1&2 next page).**
2. Use an abbreviated backswing taking the racket back at shoulder level into the classic throwing position **(see figs 3&4 next page).** This may be with the wrist cocked or the racket pointing skyward. Both are acceptable.
3. Point to the ball with the left hand, this being essential for balance and sighting the ball in. Get the left hand up as soon as you see the lob going up, this will ensure early preparation, a good sideways stance and good rhythm and timing. By bending your place up arm at the elbow you can protect your eyes with your hand if the sun is a problem.
4. Get yourself into a position under the ball. Position yourself by either **a)** moving backwards in a sideways stepping or skipping motion or **b)** cross stepping where the foot nearest the net moves in front of the rear foot before the rear foot steps back and the process is repeated.
5. Stretch up fully to the ball making sure not to let the ball drop too low **(see fig 5, next page)**
6. Contact the back of the ball with a straight or flat racket head and follow through with the racket on either the left or right side of the body.

PRACTICE METHODS.

1. Position yourself just inside the "T".
2. When learning the smash turn sideways to the net, holding your racket in a back-scratch position.
Have your hitting partner feed you easy lobs making sure to keep your feet around shoulder width and still during the hit. Transfer you weight on to your front foot during the forward swing. Start with one bounce smashes before trying to hit them in the air.
3. Practice the above, but this time take your racket back with the abbreviated backswing as described in the technique section above.
4. As you become more advanced practice some smashes starting from the volley ready position halfway between the service line and the net. Use the following 1,2,3 combination.
A) back-stepping with the right foot.
B) stepping forward and across with the left before
C) stepping forwards into the smash with the right foot.
5. Practice the above, but with faster and deeper lobs, so you are forced to back-step, jump and smash. Here make sure to take a long last step so as get the necessary spring into the jump **(photos 1,2,3,4 next page).**

Have your hitting partner play alternate drives and lobs forcing you to move forwards for the volley before forcing you back for the smash. This can also be used as a conditioning drill where you must run forwards and touch the net after each smash.

STANDING SMASH

fig 1 fig 2 fig 3 fig 4 fig 5 fig 6

PHOTO 1

PHOTO 2

JUMP SMASH

PHOTO 3

PHOTO 4

TACTICAL CONSIDERATIONS

1. The smash is the ultimate offensive shot, you can demoralize an opponent with a good overhead.

2. If the lob is deep, don't go for a full blooded smash. A relaxed, well timed and 3/4 paced smash will suffice.

3. If the smash is close to the net hit it as hard as you like, but make sure to snap the wrist to keep the ball down.

4. If the lob is high and deep let it bounce first and apply slice to a 3/4 pace well placed shot.

5. If the lob is placed well over to your backhand side apply topspin to the smash by throwing the racket face up and over the ball. Again go for positioning here **(see topspin smash figs below)**.

6. If the lob is placed well over your backhand with a lower trajectory, play a backhand smash. This demands a strong shoulder turn causing your back to be opposite the net. To achieve power your racket must meet the ball squarely and you must use a strong wrist snap. **(See backhand smash figs below).**

TOPSPIN SMASH

BACKHAND SMASH

BEGINNER, INTERMEDIATE AND ADVANCED SINGLES AND DOUBLES TACTICS

I will start this section with a basic introduction to singles and doubles tactics for the beginner. However, before I begin I'll start with a quote from the great Ivan Lendl. This can be applied to players at all levels: "Don't assume that because you beat Sam and Sam thrashes Harry, you'll mop up Harry. Match-ups are very important in tennis. What is called for naturally is an adjustment in your game which may demand that you revert to a pattern you are not at home with."

BEGINNER SINGLES TACTICS

1. Play steady, making sure to keep your percentage of placements high in relation to your errors. Try to maintain a good length of shot, making sure to play lots of looped deep drives, effective for keeping your opponent well behind the baseline.

2. Get the ball into play on your first serve and try to get the ball to your opponent's backhand.

3. Learn a drop shot and how to play it effectively, i.e. off a short ball or when your opponent is out of position.

4. If you have no confidence in your volley, then stay away from the net. Come in only on the very shortest ball where your momentum carries you so far forward that you can't retreat.

5. Never remain in "no-man's land", i.e. the area running from the service line to halfway between the service line and baseline.

6. Learn an effective defensive lob and the right time to use it.

7. Try to move your opponent around the court and play lots of cross-court drives, thus giving yourself more court to hit into.

BEGINNER DOUBLES TACTICS

1. After serving, be prepared to rally cross-court until you receive a short ball at which time you should approach the net.

2. Keep these cross-court drives well clear of both the net and the net man.

3. Learn to serve to the backhand.

4. As a variation, lob over the net man and then come in.

5. If you are pulled up to the net, don't get too close, otherwise you will be lobbed. Don't remain in no man's land after being pulled up for a short ball. Preferably join your partner up at the net, but don't be afraid to retreat backwards if you feel your volley is particularly weak.

6. If on a very short ball your momentum carries you forward to the net, stay there and attempt to volley.

7. If the ball is moving toward the opposing net player, then back up a few feet and move toward the center of the court. This increases your chance to react to the ball which will probably be directed between you and your partner or at your feet.

8. If the ball is lobbed over your head, switch sides with your partner and let him take the shot. Drop back a few feet to just in front of the service line in case your opponent poaches.

9. If the ball is in the center of the court, move over and try to intercept.

INTERMEDIATE/ADVANCED SINGLES TACTICS

1. Court positioning: during a baseline rally a good position to try to maintain is around 1 metre (three feet) behind the baseline, but this is likely to vary according to the court surface and how much topspin your opponent is applying to the ball. If your opponent is continually hitting short then stand on the baseline and cover the court from there. In general slide to the opposite side of where the ball lands when on the baseline. When at the net stay the same side as the ball **(See court positioning figs 1,2,3 next page).** Get into the habit of moving backward and forward in relation to the baseline. This helps to disrupt your opponent's depth perception, so leading to more errors from him.

2. When attacked from the net make sure to keep the ball low, thus forcing the attacker to volley upwards.

3. Play the percentages, i.e. play the tactics, shot or sequence of shots which offer you the greatest chance of winning a particular point.

4. Watch the ball very closely, learn to hit the falling ball, the ball at the top of its bounce and the ball on the rise. Most importantly learn the correct time to play such types of balls.

5. When you have a clear shot at a winner, go for it, or when that gap appears play into it and attack the net.

6. Find your opponent's weakness and exploit it, often the backhand side at club level. However, be careful not to repeat the same shot over and over, this could make his weakness strong. Sometimes you have to play to a strength to get to a weakness, e.g. hitting out wide to the forehand and then going deep to the backhand corner. Play to the strength on your terms.

7. Dictate to the ball. Don't choose the shot suggested by the speed and the path of the oncoming ball. Choose the shot which puts your opponent in the greatest danger.

8. Don't always play the obvious shot. Playing a **shot behind an opponent** into an area from which he has just started moving away is often very effective against someone who is particularly fast footed.

9. Work hard to break you opponent's service. Develop your returns and learn to drive them instead of continually blocking. If you can learn to break repeatedly it eases the pressure of having to hold your own serve and dramatically undermines your opponent's confidence.

10. Know how to move your opponent up and back. Many players don't move forward as well as they do to the side and many players will stay glued to the baseline because they have no volley. Try some floaters to force them far back beyond the baseline, then drop shot them or chip some balls around the service line, with lobs mixed in to follow.

11. If your opponent is continually pulling you up to the net, you can do the same to him. Four good ways to counter the short ball are **A)** drop shot back yourself. **B)** attack and go to the net. **C)** play short and deep down the middle. **D)** work some short angles.

12. Go to the net frequently if you have a strong wind at your back.

13. Get to know the critical points in every game, i.e. the first and third points. Also work hard to win the set up points, particularly those deuce points that take you within one point of winning the game.

14. Get to know the dictate games in a match. These are the first games in every set, the 5th, 7th and 9th games or any game that can move you within one game of the set. At such times you must raise your level of performance by intensifying your game and level of concentration. You might start by taking the ball earlier, improving the quality of your shots and keeping unforced errors to an absolute minimum.

15. Try to be aware of what your opponent is thinking. If he's getting mad at himself or the conditions you know he is probably close to quitting and there should be no problem in closing out the match. However, always be aware that players often play looser when down so make sure to keep your intensity high when closing out the match.

16. If you are losing, be ready to change your tactics. You should always have a back up plan in case your original game plan isn't working.

17. Try to win points in bunches. Go for two and three points at a time.

18. Don't be afraid to make minor adjustments to your own technique if necessary. Play at a match tempo that suits you.

19. Learn how best to play tie breaks: get off to a good start and play each point at a time.

COURT POSITIONING

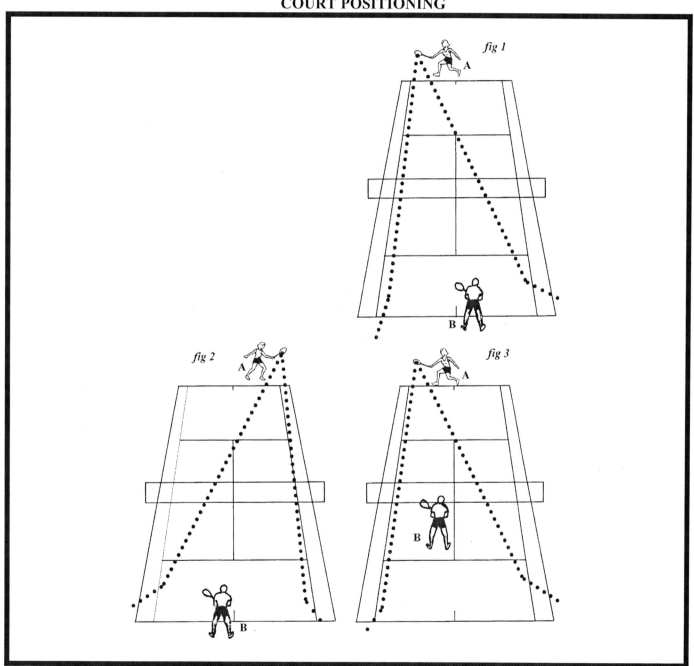

INTERMEDIATE/ADVANCED DOUBLES TACTICS

1. Become well acquainted with the basic positions on the court. When you are serving your partner should be halfway between the net and the service line in the center of his half of the court. You should serve from the center of your half and follow your serve to the net.

2. When receiving stand in the corner as for a singles return and move quickly sideways so as to cover your half of the court. Your partner should be centrally located on the service line ready to cover his half.

3. Always try to get to the net nearer and more quickly than your opponents so that you can hit down while they are forced to hit up.

4. Keep your ground strokes low over the net to protect against your opponent's volleys, particularly on returns of serve.

5. Concentrate your attack on the weaker player of the two and exploit any obvious weaknesses such as a weak overhead.

6. Keep up a high percentage of first serves and work hard to hold your own serve.

7. Intercept any weak returns as frequently as possible.

8. Develop an understanding with your partner and communicate the entire match. Develop signals which indicate to your partner your intentions, (e.g. this could be your hand pointing to the center behind your back indicating an attempt at a cross over. A clenched fist could indicate that you wish to stay).

9. Master the Australian formation which helps to protect against good consistent cross court returning. Here the server's partner stays on the same side of court as the server. The server's starting position is close to the center of the baseline enabling him to quickly cross to the other side of the court and approach the net on his opponent's down the line side.

10. Always try to stay together as a unit, i.e. when moving up and back and forced out wide. You can imagine being roped together with your partner if you like.

11. Make clear quick calls such as "mine" or "yours" to indicate who is to take a shot positioned close to both of you. Elect who is to take the down the middle shots.

12. Make quick, clean cross overs, don't get stuck with both of you on the same side of the court at the same time.

13. Serve frequently down the middle so as to give your partner regular opportunities to intercept. If your partner serves out wide make sure to take one step across to cover the down the line.

14. If you are struggling when receiving, try moving back on the baseline together and play down the middle.

15. When all four players are at the net play down the middle and attack the weaker player or the player nearest you.

16. Remember that when returning in doubles you have five possibilities: **A)** the lob over the net man. **B)** the drive down the middle. **C)** the chipped advance. **D)** the drive down the alley. **E)** the drive straight at the net man.

CHOOSING A GAME

Try to develop your tennis hand in hand with what fits into your physical, mental and temperamental make up. You should fall into at least one of the following categories.
1. The all courter
2. The serve volleyer
3. The aggressive baseliner
4. The counter punching baseliner

1. THE ALL COURTER

The all courter is the most adaptable of the four and has the ability to play well in all parts of the court. His or her ground strokes are normally solid with good volleys to back them up. This player has a great ability to adapt to the court surface being played on and to the type of opponent being played against. Good examples of great all court players are Roger Federer pictured opposite and Justine Henin-Hardenne pictured below.

ROGER FEDERER

**JUSTINE
HENIN-HARDENNE**

.THE SERVE VOLLEYER

Always has a strong first and second serve, great volleys, overheads and the ability to move forward and backward tremendously well. He or she has excellent approach shots, great reactions and a natural ability to anticipate the next shot from the opponent. A good serve and volleyer in form is a very tough opponent to beat because your are continually pressured to come up with great shots to win the point. Tim Henman pictured opposite is a great serve volleyer.

TIM HENMAN

3. THE AGGRESSIVE BASELINER

The typical aggressive baseliner often has a couple of big shots, often a big first serve and a big forehand. Rather than react in a point, this type of player likes to dictate from the back of the court. This player will hit a lot of clean winners and will generate mistakes from the opponent by the shear weight of stroke. He or she will most often be physically strong and will be seeking the short ball to attack. Good examples of great aggressive baseliners are Serena Williams pictured opposite and Rafael Nadal pictured below.

SERENA WILLIAMS

RAFAEL NADAL

GUILLERMO CORIA

4. THE COUNTER PUNCHING BASELINER

He or she is the classic reactor and will patiently wait for the opponent to do something before coming up with the counter. This type of player is normally extremely fit and mentally tough, endowed with solid ground strokes, great returns and often great movement. He or she will most often be equipped with great passing shots and topspin lobs. Patience and perseverance are this player's main virtues. A great counter puncher is Guillermo Coria, pictured opposite.

PRE-MATCH PREPARATION

All tennis players feel a certain degree of pre-match tension going into a match, but there are certain methods that can help to dispel such tensions.

1. One idea is to go into a match with one or two single goals. For example in the past you know you had trouble hitting out on your backhand under pressure. Now your goal might be to hit out, when in the same situation in the past you hit a weak slice or lob. Focusing on this goal will help keep out distracting thoughts of winning and losing, thoughts which often inhibit performance. Setting specific goals can also help you improve faster, i.e. by focusing on particulars.

2. By preparing meticulously you can help to reduce tension. Make a thorough check of your equipment well before leaving for the match. For example make sure that you have two or three rackets strung up to their optimum playing tension. The more successful player learns to eliminate as many elements of uncertainty as possible before stepping out on the court. The player can then focus exclusively on the task at hand. Correct tournament preparation can start weeks, days or hours before the event. This preparation can be split into 3 categories: **1. Procedural preparation 2. Physical preparation 3. Mental preparation**

1. PROCEDURAL PREPARATION

Your procedural preparation may begin as you start thinking about the match and your opponent before you leave your house. You can be thinking of your match strategy and positive thoughts about your approach to the match. In the days or even weeks leading up to the match you should gear your practice to the court surface that you will be playing on. If it is a particularly fast surface try to practice on a fast court and work hard on your serve, volley and approach shot techniques. If you get a chance to scout your opponent, then do so. You might have played him before, so here is the perfect opportunity to prepare an efficient game plan. Try to practice with weaker partners so that you can work on new techniques and stronger partners so you will be tested more competitively. Always do some drills before you play the practice sets. Be careful not to practice too much or too little, find that optimum practice amount. Always make sure to get to the event site at least half an hour before the start time, this will give you plenty of time to check in with the organizers and get familiar with the surroundings. This will help you to feel more at ease at the start of the match. If your opponent turns up late and is feeling rushed at the start this could be worth an early lead in the first set.

The following is a list of items that should be included in your tennis bag: water plus a good sports drink such as Gatorade; rackets: two or three well strung frames and spare overwraps (grips); muscle spray; spare shirts and socks; warm up suit; towels; ice Pack; dampeners (elastic bands); potassium pills or bananas (anti cramping); caps; headband and sweat bands; surgical tape; sun glasses; extra shoes; sun-screen; notepad with pre-written ideas on the match, which could be reviewed at the change overs if necessary, plus a pencil to record any new ideas.

2. PHYSICAL PREPARATION

Always try some stretches before the pre-match warm up. If possible, try to get a practice hit 15 to 20 minutes before the match. Break a sweat and relieve some of that pre-match tension. You should have done at least 30 minutes of stretching before you left the house so that you are ready to go when you get there. Take a good look at your opponent in the pre-match warm up. If you know nothing about him you can quickly build up a plan around your general plan of tactics on this particular surface. Analyse information such as the following: What spins does he prefer to hit with? Does he run around his backhand? Is his serve looking particularly good or not?

Make sure to vary the spin and positioning on your serve and try to swing at some returns in the warm up. Get 'springy' on the balls of your feet and keep them moving. As you rally from the baseline draw in a deep breath as you take the racket back and exhale as you contact the ball and follow through. Watch the seems of the ball, sing a song to yourself, anything that settles you down and helps you to focus on the task at hand. At the start of the match don't necessarily serve first if you win the toss. If it's very windy try hitting into the wind at the start. If it's very sunny then keep the sun at your back. Try to establish a smooth early rhythm, gradually working your way up through the gears. Always make sure to utilize the first change over by calming yourself and reviewing your game plan. What do you want to happen and what do you want to prevent from happening?

3. MENTAL PREPARATION

When you stretch briefly before the warm up take some good deep breaths and review your positive thinking and visualization techniques used over the preceding days and weeks. Such techniques should be practiced 10 to 15 minutes each night in the days and weeks preceding the event. You can, for example, visualize yourself playing well, winning point after point, playing according to techniques, tactics and strategies you have been working on in practice. You can even imagine yourself shaking hands with your beaten opponent, try anything that works for you. At tense times in a match use deep breathing to calm yourself and make sure not to rush. During the change overs relax and review your strategy, go over your game plan in your mind. Don't look outside the court and be distracted by anything. Look at the ground between points or at your racket. Try to develop a routine to keep the mind occupied. Play one point at a time and don't let a bad point or call pray on your mind. Think positively and focus on the next point. You can't afford to waist mental energy by focusing on something that happened two or three points back. Champions know that the net cords and bad calls tend to even out during a match and they have the ability to channel their anger and emotion into the game. They are under control; lose your temper and you'll probably end up losing the match. Work hard on improving your all round concentration ability, both on and off the court. Good concentration is vital if you are to become a top player.

DRILLS

INTRODUCTION

All serious practice sessions should start with some drills. This section gives a good variety of singles and doubles drills which I hope you will enjoy. When drilling it really gives you a chance to improve technique, movement and consistency before you play more competitive practice sets and matches. Always try and maintain a good balance between the drilling and more competitive side of training sessions.

GROUNDSTROKE DRILLS.

1A. Forehand crosscourt. Both players A&B start at the baseline and rally forehand to forehand making sure to get back to the centre after each shot.

1B. Backhand crosscourt. Same as above, but now on the backhand side.

2A Forehand down the line. Both players A&B start at the baseline and rally down the line A hitting forehands and B backhands.

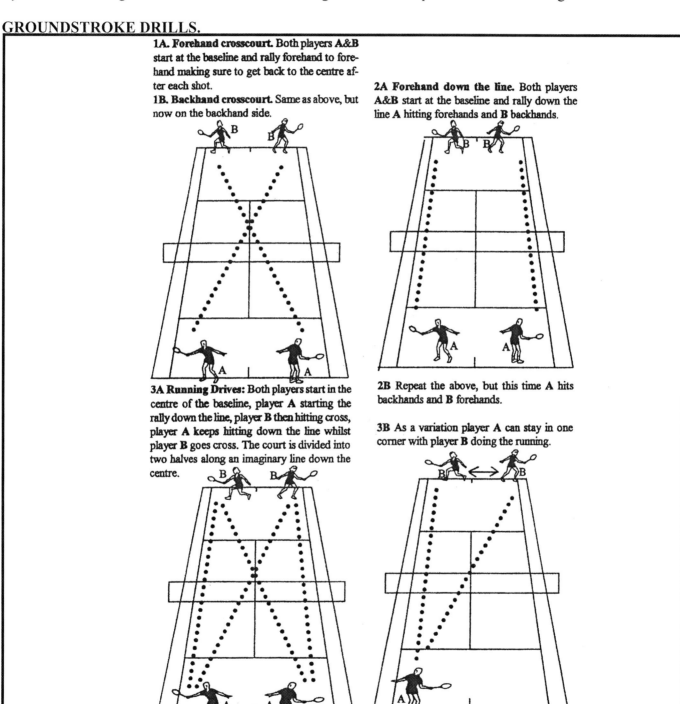

3A Running Drives: Both players start in the centre of the baseline, player A starting the rally down the line, player B then hitting cross, player A keeps hitting down the line whilst player B goes cross. The court is divided into two halves along an imaginary line down the centre.

2B Repeat the above, but this time A hits backhands and B forehands.

3B As a variation player A can stay in one corner with player B doing the running.

4. Hitting down the tramlines. a) Forehand to backhand. Players **A** and **B** stand in the corners of the singles court, **A**, hitting forehands and **B**, hitting backhands down the line, line 1 **b)** Backhand to forehand, as above line 2

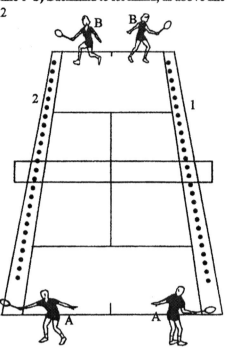

5. Depth drill. Players **A** & **B** rally Forehands and backhands up and down concentrating on hitting a good length. Use depth markers such as 4 tennis balls to mark the required depths.

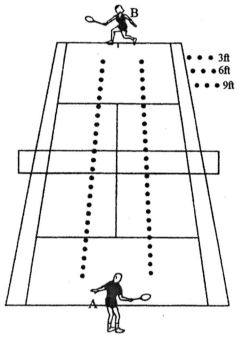

6. Consistency drill. Players **A** & **B** rally back and forth at a good steady pace with the aim of keeping the ball going as long as possible.

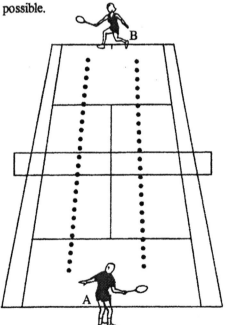

7. Power drill. Players **A** & **B** hit balls from the baseline all over the court Player **A** trying to hit winners all the time player **B** just returning everything.

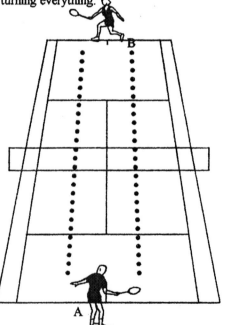

VOLLEY CONTROL DRILLS.

1A. Forehand Crosscourt Volley. Player A is on the baseline and rallies crosscourt Forehand. drives to Player B who hits crosscourt Forehand volleys. **1B. Backhand Crosscourt volleys.** the same as above, but on the backhand.

2A. Backhand Down The Line Volleys. Player A hits Forehand drives to B who hits backhand volleys down the line.
2B. Forehand down the line volleys. The same as above, but forehand volleys down the line.

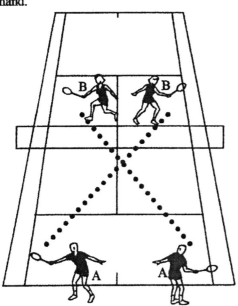 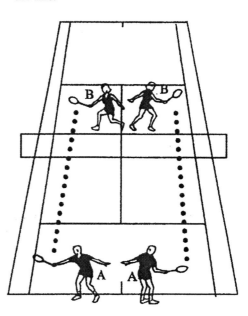

3. Volley - Volley. **a)** Players A & B halfway between the net and the service line rally forehand and backhand volleys back and forth. *Variations* a) both players rally low volleys. *b)* both players volley from service line

4. Players A & B stand halfway between the net and service line and practice crosscourt volleys, first forehand, then backhand. Use the same variations as mentioned in **3.**

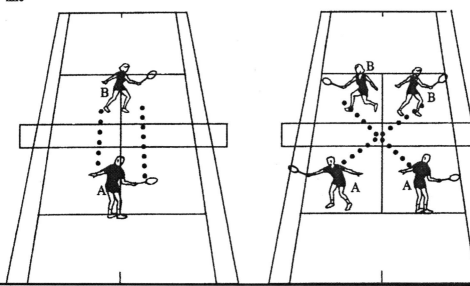

83

DOUBLES DRILLS.

1. Ghost Doubles. (*For 2 Players*) **A** serves to **B** and the point is played out cross court. Player **A** may serve and volley or stay back.

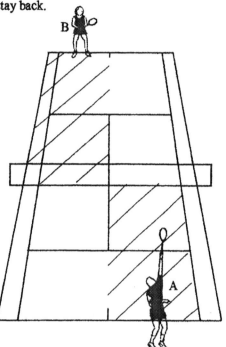

2. Defend the net. Players **A** & **B** start at the net, either player starting the rally with an under arm feed. **C** or **D** returns with a drive. The point is then played out.

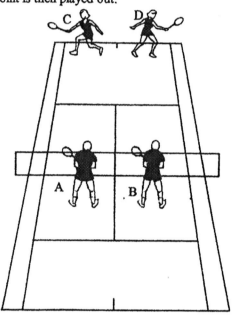

3. Attackers v Defenders. Both pairs start at the back and rally until the attacking pairs's ball lands inside the service line. Here they must approach and then the point is played out

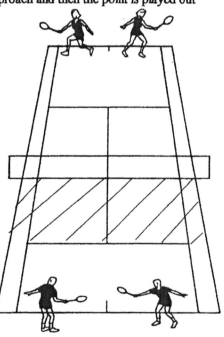

4. Short court serve and volley attacker v defender. Player **A** serves halfway between the service line and baseline and joins his partner at the net. Normal game scoring can be used here.

5. Down the Middle Serve return Intercept.
A serves down the middle, C returns towards the middle giving **B** an opportunity to intercept.

6. Australian Formation. A serves with his partner in an attacking volley position on his side of the court. A moves over to B's original side after serving. **D** is forced to return down the line.

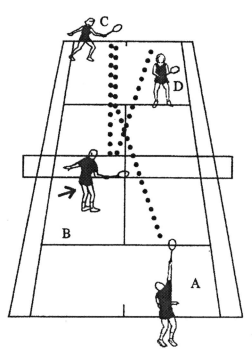

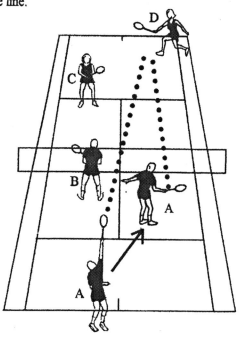

7. Returners Partner intercept. A serve's C returns and **D** intercepts A's first volley

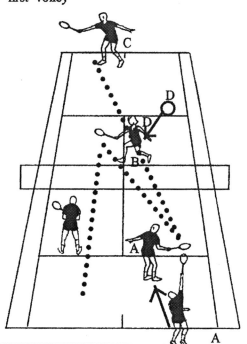

SERVICE AND RETURN DRILLS.

1A Player **A** is serving and Player **B** returning forehands and backhands Player **A** serves only one type of serve e.g. flat or he can mix up his serves.

1B player **A** serves from halfway between the service line and the baseline and **B** again returns one type of serve or a mixture.

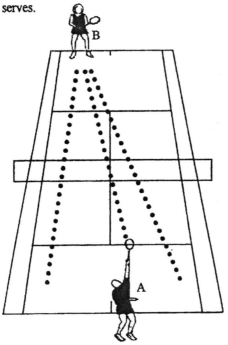

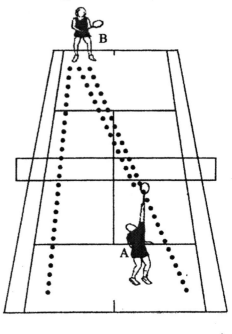

2A As a variation **A** serves straight down one half of the court and **B** returns into a more confined area. Half court singles:-Here the point is played out after the serve, mini matches can be played to 11 or 21, a very effective exercise.

2B Here **A** moves forwards to halfway between the service line and the baseline and does the same. As a variation play half court singles, serve and volley.

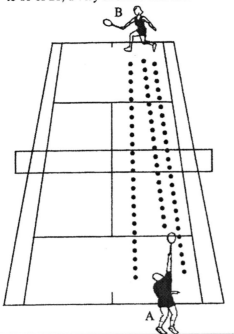

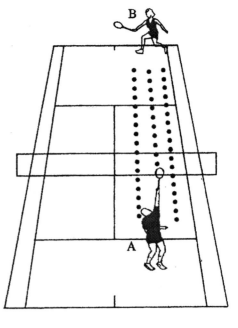

SIMULATION DRILLS WITH TARGETS.

1A. Inside out Forehand drill. Player A feeds B to his backhand side B runs around the backhand and hits an inside out forehand to A's backhand side, As a variation B can blast the ball down the line on every 3rd ball.

1B. As a variation A feeds the first ball wide to B's Forehand corner, B hits down the line A feeds the next ball to B's backhand side B runs across & around the backhand, hitting either target.

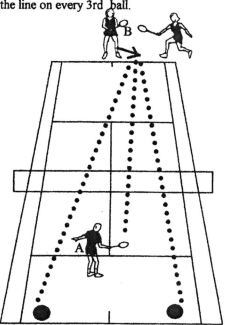

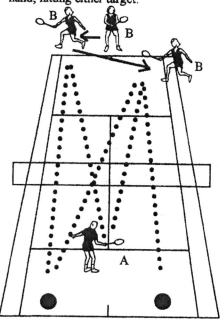

2. Drop Shot Lob Drill.
Both players A & B start on the baseline , player A starting the rally with a short ball, B moves forward & plays a drop player A advances and B plays a lob.

3. Passing shot drill.
A starts at thy net, B at the baseline. Both rally down the line until A hits cross court B runs across & hits a down the line passing shot. Use a towel on the net as a target.

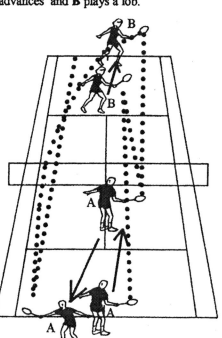

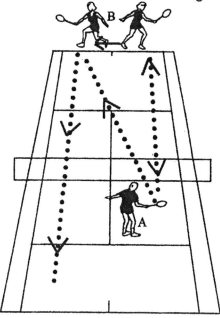

SMASH AND LOB DRILLS

1. Lob Smash consistency drill.

A stands on the baseeline and **B** at the T junction. A lobs and **B** smashes at 3/4 speed. The same drill can be practised 1/2 court.

2. Overheads placement drill.

A stands on the baseline and feeds **B** smashes which must be hit at the corner targets.

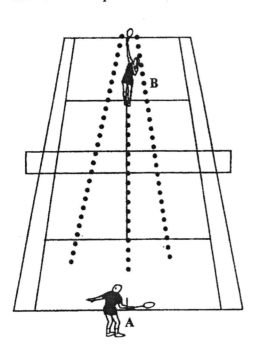 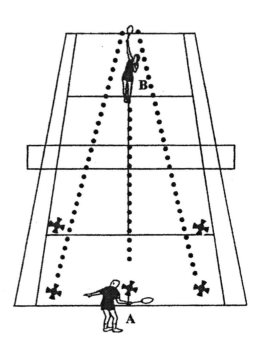

3. Forehand Volley, Backhand Volley, Smash Drill.

A stands on the baseline and feeds **B** a forehand volley *(line 1)*, a backhand volley *(line 2)* and a smash. *(line 3)*

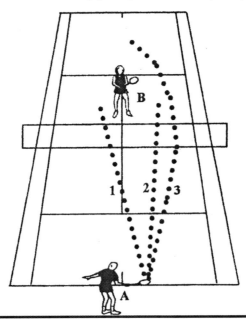

FITNESS

INTRODUCTION
The hard demands of modern day tennis mean tennis players have to be fitter and stronger than ever before. This section will cover the four main areas of tennis fitness including:
1. The warm up and suppleness
2. Strength
3. Stamina
4. Speed and Agility

1. THE WARM UP AND SUPPLENESS EXERCISES
Stretching is vital before any physical exercise, helping you to tune the body physically and mentally. Proper stretching will prevent muscle tears from the tendinous attachments and enable the performer to exercise vigorously without fear of injury. The following changes take place in the body after a proper warm up period:
1. Viscosity within the muscle is decreased, thus allowing the muscle to contract and relax with greater speed.
2. Blood flow is increased to the muscles due to blood vessel dilatation.
3. With increased blood flow oxygen supply is also increased.
4. Heart rate, blood pressure, respiratory rate are also increased and more energy producing nutrients are carried to the muscles and waste products are eliminated faster.
5. A temperature rise in active muscles.

Before stretching make sure to jog for a few minutes beforehand, even on the same spot. This really helps to get the blood circulating. Then proceed to work systematically through all parts of the body: neck, shoulders, arms, chest, trunk, hips and legs. Repeat each movement 5 to10 times gradually increasing the effort. Stretch gradually, hold for a second or two, don't bounce, then relax and repeat. For rolling exercises rotate the part on as wide an arc as possible. Develop a full range of movements for work at home **(see fig below)**. Also develop a short set of stretches for a quick court work out.

SPINE, HIPS AND HAMSTRINGS

1. SIDE BENDS   **2. TRUNK TWISTS**   **3. ALTERNATE TOE TOUCHES**

4. NECK ROLLS

SHOULDERS AND UPPER BODY

5. WING STRETCHES   **6. ARM CIRCLES**   **7. ARM FLINGS**

ABDOMEN, THIGHS AND CALVES

8. THE REACH   **9. THE LUNGE**   **10. HURDLES**

UPPER AND LOWER LEGS

11. LEG SWINGS   **12. KNEE PULLS**   **13. CALF STRETCHES**

2. STRENGTH EXERCISES

HOUSEHOLD EXERCISES
The following exercises are designed to strengthen muscles and ligaments and by the use of high repetition to improve muscle endurance. They can be done in the house or the gym or practically anywhere.

1. Press ups
Lying on the floor face downwards, feet together and hands under the shoulders, push the body off the floor by straightening the arms. Then lower the body to the floor by bending the arms, it is important to keep the back straight. As a variation use the fingers instead of the flat of the hands.

2. Hip raises
Sitting on the floor with legs and feet together and hands placed flat on the ground, raise the body using only the hands, until the arms are straight. Hold for a count of 5, then relax and repeat. The body should be vertical and arms completely straight when raised from the floor. By placing a book or books under the hands the exercise can be made more difficult. Again as a variation use the finger tips.

3. Tennis ball squeeze
Squeeze as hard as you can on a tennis ball and hold for a count of 5 and then relax.

4. Bicycling
Lying on the back as shown opposite carry out a cycling movement with the legs. Pull back the knee as far towards the face as comfortable, then straighten it fully.

5. Bent leg sit ups
Lying on the back, legs bent and arms to the side with the feet under a low bar, wardrobe, chair, sofa or someone holding the ankles. Raise the body slowly to a sitting position leaning forward, trying to touch the knees with the head. Then slowly return to the sitting position.

PRESS UPS

HIP RAISES

BICYLING

BENT LEG SIT UPS

6. Squat Thrusts

Start as shown in the illustration. Shoot out the legs behind you into the push up position and then bring them forward again. Keep the feet together at all times.

SQUAT THRUSTS

7. Leg raises

Lying flat on the back with hands on the floor, palms down, raise one leg slowly about 9 inches, then lower it again. Relax and repeat with the other leg.

8. Step ups

Standing up straight with hands at the sides facing the chair, stool or pile of large books 12-18 inches in height. Proceed to place the right foot on the stool and by using only the power of the legs raise the body until standing on the stool. Step down again slowly and repeat with the left leg, the body should remain upright throughout.

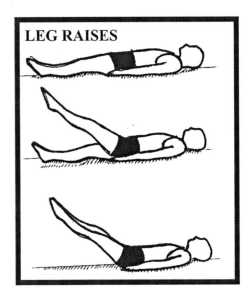

LEG RAISES

WEIGHT TRAINING

The most important aspect of strength training for tennis is that it increases speed and power. Greater force of stroke can be generated by increasing strength in the arms and shoulders. Strength work on the legs will allow more rapid movement around the court. I have listed some excellent exercises for use on any good multi gym (see next page).

First note the following points. **1.** For each exercise work on the weight resistance to use so that you can do no more than ten repetitions (for strength) and between ten and twenty reps (for muscle endurance). **2.** The number of reps you can do in one go is called a set and you should try to complete three sets in a particular training session. **3.** Each muscle group must be rested after each set. **4.** Try to do at least 3 sessions per week initially for most rapid improvement, particularly when you are not involved in regular match play. Then keep going with one or two sessions per week to maintain your levels. Use fairly light weights for the first two weeks.

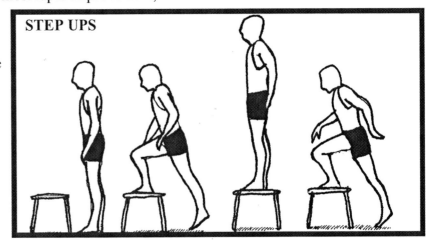

STEP UPS

MULTI GYM EXERCISES FOR TENNIS

1. HIP FLEXORS (arms straight)

2. REVERSE CURLS

3. LEG PRESS

4. CHEST PRESS

5. LEG CURLS

6. SQUAT CLEANS

7. PULL DOWNS (behind the neck)

8. LEG EXTENSIONS

9. STRAIGHT ARM PULLOVERS

10. SIDE BENDS

3. STAMINA BUILDING DRILLS

For the unfit, partially fit, or those who haven't taken exercise for some time walking is the best way to build up stamina. This should be a brisk walk with the back straight and head up. Jogging is the next progression and an excellent stamina builder. Other good stamina builders include jump rope, cycling and swimming. The preceding household strength exercises are also good stamina builders if performed with sufficiently high repetition.

1. Circuit training
Where a series of strength exercises is mixed with suppleness routines forming a circuit of exercises. With circuits always start with a warm up. No two successive exercises should work on the same part of the body, thus giving variety. The training program must be progressive and comprehensive. Within these guide lines the choice is a wide one and entirely personal. A good example would be as follows.

Arm circles (sup 6)
Bent leg sit ups (strength 5)
Knee pulls (sup14)
Squat thrusts (strength 6)
Hip rises (strength 2)
Leg swings (sup 13)
Push ups (strength 1)
Alternate toe touches (sup 3)
The lunge (sup 11)

2. Running
Continuous runs may be performed at a steady pace throughout or at a varying pace. This type of training can be used at the beginning of a training day or as the last part of a fitness session.

3. Interval running
If you have a running track or other marked out area available. The perimeter of four end on tennis courts is approx 200 metres. As an example with a length of run at 200 metres:
Number of runs 6 to 10 (increase to 10 as stamina improves).
Rest   1 minute between each run.
Target male   35 seconds per run.
Female   40 seconds per run.

4. SPEED AND AGILITY BUILDING EXERCISES

Training to improve speed and agility requires very intensive activity for fairly short periods of time. Quality of performance is of major importance and every exercise should be performed perfectly with near maximum effort. In developing speed around the court, the best training exercises involve using the court itself for sprint drills. Two of the best routines are the line drill and the ball shuttle run, outlined next page.

LINE DRILL

1. Start from the 'T' junction at the center of the court. Face the net.

2. Sidestep to the outside line.

3. Sprint to the net.

4. Sidestep across to the opposite side line.

5. Run backwards to the baseline.

6. Sidestep across the court to the opposite side line.

7. Sprint up to the net.

8. Sidestep to the center.

9. And run backwards to finish at the 'T' junction.

This one routine covers most of the movements you need in the game. Sidestepping, back-peddling, turning and forwards sprinting. Try to use short steps when conducting this drill. Time yourself on the first run, and then keep trying to improve on your time. Repeat the exercise 5-6 times in each training session, allowing about 30 seconds rest between each run.

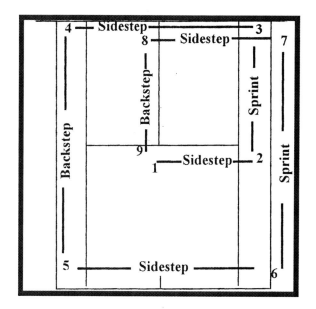

BALL SHUTTLE RUN

1. Take four balls with you on court. Put one ball on the inside tram line, one ball on the center service line, one ball on the far inside tramline and the last ball on the far sideline. Each ball should be the same distance from the net.

2. Start the drill from the sideline. Take a step or two, bend and pick up the first ball.

3. Turn and put it down where you started from.

4. Sprint to the center service line, pick up the ball, and place it with the first.

5. Collect all balls as quickly as possible, in the same manner. A good tip is to place each ball on the head of a tennis racket. This is a drill that reproduces the stop and start movements, the bending, turning and sprinting you need in a game. Again, time your first run, and try to keep improving it.

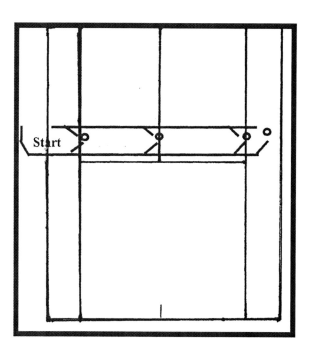

95

TENNIS COURT LAYOUT

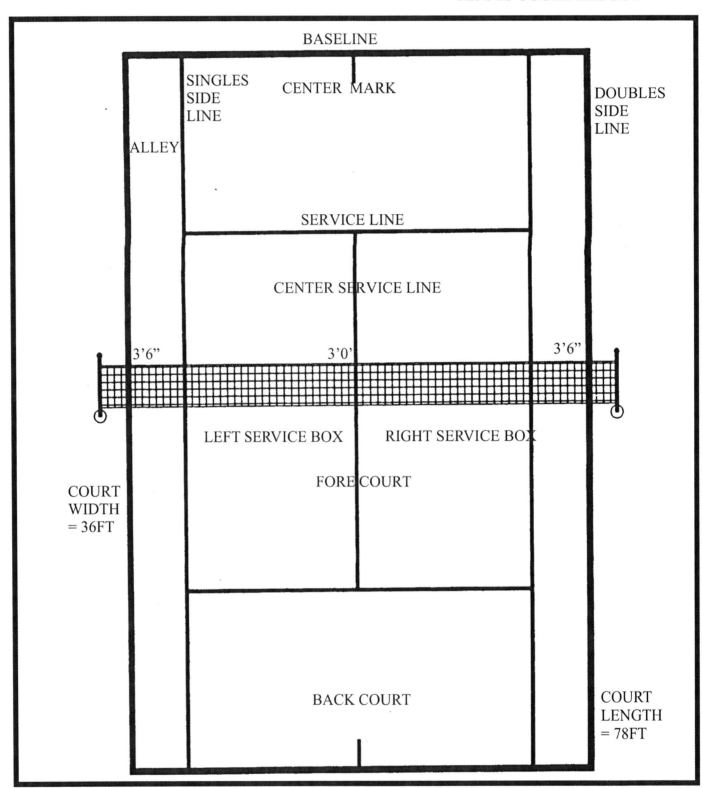

SINGLES RULES

1. **The Court** shall be a rectangle 23.77m (78ft) long and 8.23m (27ft) wide. It shall be divided across the middle by a net suspended from a cord or metal cable of a maximum diameter of 0.8cm (one-third of an inch), the ends of which shall be attached to, or pass over, the tops of the two posts, which shall be not more than 15cm (6in) square or 15cm (6in) in diameter. These posts shall not be higher than 2.5cm (1in) above the top of the net cord. The centres of the posts shall be .914m (3ft) outside the Court on each side and the height of the posts shall be such that the top of the cord or metal cable shall be 1.07m (3ft 6in) above the ground.

When a combined doubles (see Rule 34) and singles Court with a doubles net is used for singles, the net must be supported to a height of 1.07m (3ft 6in) by means of two posts, called "singles sticks", which shall be not more than 7.5cm (3in) square or 7.5cm (3in) in diameter. The centres of the singles sticks shall be .914m (3ft) outside the singles Court on each side.

The net shall be extended fully so that it fills completely the space between the two posts and shall be of sufficiently small mesh to prevent the ball passing through. The height of the net shall be .914m (3ft) at the centre, where it shall be held down taut by a strap not more than 5cm (2in) wide and completely white in colour. There shall be a band covering the cord or metal cable and the top of the net of not less than 5cm (2in) nor more than 6.3cm (2½in) in depth on each side and completely white in colour. There shall be no advertisement on the net, strap band or singles sticks.

The lines bounding the ends and sides of the Court shall respectively be called the base-lines and the side-lines. On each side of the net, at a distance of 6.40m (21ft) from it and parallel with it, shall be drawn the service-lines. The space on each side of the net between the service-line and the side-lines shall be divided into two equal parts called the service-courts by the centre service-line, which must be 5cm (2in) in width, drawn half-way between, and parallel with, the side-line. Each base-line shall be bisected by an imaginary continuation of the centre service-line to a line 10cm (4in) in length and 5cm (2in) in width called "the centre mark" drawn inside the Court, at right angles to and in contact with such base-lines. All other lines shall not be less than 2.5cm (1in) nor more than 5cm (2in) in width, except the base-line, which may be 10cm (4in) in width, and all measurements shall be made to the outside of the lines.

All lines shall be of uniform colour. If advertising or any other material is placed at the back of the Court, it may not contain white, or yellow. A light colour may only be used if this does not interfere with the vision of the players. If advertisements are placed on the chairs of the linesmen sitting at the back of the Court, they may not contain white or yellow. A light colour may only be used if this does not interfere with the vision of the players.

Note: In the case of the *Davis Cup* or other Official Championships of the International Tennis Federation, there shall be a space behind each base-line of not less than 6.4m (21ft), and at the sides of not less than 3.66m (12ft). The chairs of linesmen may be placed at the back of a Court within the 6.4m (21ft) or at the side of the court within the 3.66m (12ft), provided they do not protrude into that area more than .914m (3ft).

2. The **permanent fixtures** of the Court shall include not only the net, posts, singles sticks, cord or metal cable, strap and band, but also, where there are any such, the back and side stops, the stands, fixed or movable seats and chairs round the Court, and their occupants, all other fixtures around and above the Court, and the Umpire, Net-cord Judge, Footfault Judge, Linesmen and Ball Boys when in their respective places.

Note: For the purpose of this Rule, the word "Umpire" comprehends the Umpire, the persons entitled to a seat on the Court, and all those persons designated to assist the Umpire in the conduct of a match.

3. **The Ball** shall have a uniform outer surface and shall be white or yellow in colour. If there are any seams they shall be stitchless. The ball shall be more than 6.35cm (two and a half inches) and less than 6.67cm (two and five-eighths inches) in diameter, and more than 56.7 grams (two ounces) and less than 58.5 grams (two and one-sixteenth ounces) in weight. The ball shall have a bound of more than 135cm (53in) and less than 147cm (58in) when dropped 254cm (100in) upon a concrete base. The ball shall have a forward deformation of more than .56cm (.220 of an inch) and less than .74cm (.290 of an inch) and a return deformation of more than .89cm (.350 of an inch) and less than 1.08cm (.425 of an inch) at 8.165kg (18lb) load. The two deformation figures shall be the average of three individual readings along three axes of the ball and no two individual readings shall differ by more than .08cm (.030 of an inch) in each case.

For play above 1219m (4,000ft) in altitude above sea level, two additional types of ball may be used. The first type is identical to those described above except that the bound shall be more than 121.92cm (48in) and less than 135cm (53in) and shall have an internal pressure that is greater than the external pressure. This type of tennis ball is commonly known as a pressurized ball. The second type is identical to those described above except that they shall have a bound of more than 135cm (53in) and less than 147cm (58in) and shall have an internal pressure that is approximately equal to the external pressure and have been acclimatized for 60 days or more at the altitude of the specific tournament. This type of tennis ball is commonly known as a zero-pressure or non-pressurized ball.

All tests for bound, size and deformation shall be in accordance with the regulations in Appendix I.

4 The Racket Rackets failing to comply with the following specifications are not approved for play under the Rules of Tennis:
(a) The hitting surface of the racket shall be flat and consist of a pattern of crossed strings connected to a frame and alternately interlaced or bonded where they cross; and the stringing pattern shall be generally uniform, and in particular not less dense in the centre than in any other area. The strings shall be free of attached objects and protrusions other than those utilized solely and specifically to limit or prevent wear and tear or vibration, and which are reasonable in size and placement for such purposes.
(b) The frame of the racket shall not exceed 81.28cm (32in) in overall length, including the handle and 31.75cm (12$\frac{1}{2}$in) in overall width. The strung surface shall not exceed 39.37cm (15$\frac{1}{2}$in) in overall length, and 29.21cm (11$\frac{1}{2}$in) in overall width.
(c) The frame, including the handle, shall be free of attached objects and devices other than those utilized solely and specifically to limit or prevent wear and tear or vibration, or to distribute weight. Any objects and devices must be reasonable in size and placement for such purposes.
(d) The frame, including the handle, and the strings, shall be free of any device which makes it possible to change materially the shape of the racket, or to change the weight distribution, during the playing of a point. The International Tennis Federation shall rule on the question of whether any racket or prototype complies with the above specifications or is otherwise approved, or not approved, for play.

5 Server & Receiver The players shall stand on opposite sides of the net; the player who first delivers the ball shall be called the Server, and the other the Receiver.

6 Choice of Ends & Service The choice of ends and the right to be Server or Receiver in the first game shall be decided by toss. The player winning the toss may choose or require his opponent to choose:-
(a) The right to be Server or Receiver, in which case the other player shall choose the end; or
(b) The end, in which case the other player shall choose the right to be Server or Receiver.

7 The Service shall be delivered in the following manner. Immediately before commencing to serve, the Server shall stand with both feet at rest behind (i.e. further from the net than) the base-line, and within the imaginary continuations of the centre-mark and side-line. The Server shall then project the ball by hand into the air in any direction and before it hits the ground strike it with his racket, and the delivery shall be deemed to have been completed at the moment of the impact of the racket and the ball. A player with the use of only one arm may utilize his racket for the projection.

8 Foot Fault (a) The Server shall throughout the delivery of the Service:-

(i) Not change his position by walking or running. The Server shall not by slight movements of the feet which do not materially affect the location originally taken up by him, be deemed "to change his position by walking or running".
(ii) Not touch, with either foot, any area other than that behind the base-line within the imaginary extension of the centre-mark and side-lines.
(b) The word "foot" means the extremity of the leg.

9 Delivery of Service
(a) In delivering the service, the Server shall stand alternately behind the right and left Courts beginning from the right in every game. If service from a wrong half of the Court occurs and is undetected, all play resulting from such wrong service or services shall stand, but the inaccuracy of station shall be corrected immediately it is discovered.
(b) The ball served shall pass over the net and hit the ground within the Service Court which is diagonally opposite, or upon any line bounding such Court, before the Receiver returns it.

10 Service Fault The Service is a fault:
(a) If the Server commits any breach of Rules 7, 8 or 9 (b);
(b) If he misses the ball in attempting to strike it;
(c) If the ball served touches a permanent fixture (other than the net, strap or band) before it hits the ground.

11 Second Service After a fault (if it is the first fault) the Server shall serve again from behind the same half of the Court from which he served that fault, unless the service was from the wrong half, when, in accordance with Rule 9, the Server shall be entitled to one service only from behind the other half.

12 When to Serve The Server shall not serve until the Receiver is ready. If the latter attempts to return the service, he shall be deemed ready. If, however, the Receiver signifies that he is not ready, he may not claim a fault because the ball does not hit the ground within the limits fixed for the service.

13 The Let In all cases where a let has to be called under the rules, or to provide for an interruption to play, it shall have the following interpretations:-
(a) When called solely in respect of a service that one service only shall be replayed.
(b) When called under any other circumstances, the point shall be replayed.

14 The "Let" in Service The Service is a let:-
(a) If the ball served touches the net, strap or band, and is otherwise good, or, after touching the net. strap or band, touches the Receiver or anything which he wears or carries before hitting the ground.
(b) If a service or a fault is delivered when the Receiver is not ready (see Rule 12).
    In case of a let, that particular service shall not count, and the Server shall serve again, but a service let does not annul a previous fault.

15 Order of Service At the end of the first game the

Receiver shall become Server, and the Server Receiver; and so on alternately in all the subsequent games of a match. If a player serves out of turn, the player who ought to have served shall serve as soon as the mistake is discovered, but all points scored before such discovery shall be reckoned. A fault served before such discovery shall not be reckoned. If a game shall have been completed before such discovery, the order of service remains as altered.

16 **When Players Change Ends** The players shall change ends at the end of the first, third and every subsequent alternate game of each set, and at the end of each set unless the total number of games in such set is event, in which case the change is not made until the end of the first game of the next set. If a mistake is made and the correct sequence is not followed the players must take up their correct station as soon as the discovery is made and follow their original sequence.

17 **The Ball in Play** A ball is in play from the moment at which it is delivered in service. Unless a fault or a let is called it remains in play until the point is decided.

18 **Server Wins Point** The Server wins the point:-
(a) If the ball served, not being a let under Rule 14, touches the Receiver or anything which he wears or carries, before it hits the ground;
(b) If the Receiver otherwise loses the point as provided by Rule 20.

19 **Receiver Wins Point** The Receiver wins the point:-
(a) If the Server serves two consecutive faults;
(b) If the Server otherwise loses the point as provided by Rule 20.

20 **Player Loses Point** A player loses the point if:-
(a) He fails, before the ball in play has hit the ground twice consecutively, to return it directly over the net (except as provided in Rule 24 (a) or (c); or
(b) He returns the ball in play so that it hits the ground, a permanent fixture, or other object, outside any of the lines which bound his opponent's Court (except as provided in Rule 24 (a) or (c); or
(c) He volleys the ball and fails to make a good return even when standing outside the Court; or
(d) In playing the ball he deliberately carries or catches it on his racket or deliberately touches it with his racket more than once; or
(e) He or his racket (in his hand or otherwise) or anything which he wears or carries touches the net, posts, singles sticks, cord or metal cable, strap or band, or the ground within his opponent's Court at any time while the ball is in play; or
(f) He volleys the ball before it has passed the net; or
(g) The ball in play touches him or anything that he wears or carries, except his racket in his hand or hands; or
(h) He throws his racket at and hits the ball; or
(i) He deliberately and materially changes the shape of his racket during the playing of the point.

21 **Player Hinders Opponent** If a player commits any act which hinders his opponent in making a stroke, then, if this is deliberate, he shall lose the point or if involuntary, the point shall be replayed.

22 **Ball Falls on Line** A ball falling on a line is regarded as falling in the Court bounded by that line.

23 **Ball Touches Permanent Fixtures** If the ball in play touches a permanent fixture (other than the net, posts, singles sticks, cord or metal cable, strap or band) after it has hit the ground, the player who struck it wins the point; if before it hits the ground, his opponent wins the point.

24 **A Good Return** It is a good return:-
(a) If the ball touches the net, posts, singles sticks, cord or metal cable, strap or band, provided that it passes over any of them and hits the ground within the Court; or
(b) If the ball, served or returned, hits the ground within the proper Court and rebounds or is blown back over the net, and the player whose turn it is to strike reaches over the net and plays the ball, provided that neither he nor any part of his clothes or racket touches the net, posts, singles sticks, cord or metal cable, strap or band or the ground within his opponent's Court, and that the stroke be otherwise good; or
(c) If the ball is returned outside the posts, or singles sticks, either above or below the level of the top to the net, even though it touches the posts or singles sticks, provided that it hits the ground within the proper Court; or
(d) If a player's racket passes over the net after he has returned the ball, provided the ball passes the net before being played and is properly returned; or
(e) If a player succeeds in returning the ball, served or in play, which strikes a ball lying in the Court.
Note: In a singles match, if, for the sake of convenience, a Doubles Court is equipped with singles sticks for the purpose of a singles game, then the doubles posts and those portions of the net, cord or metal cable and the band outside such singles sticks shall at all times be permanent fixtures, and are not regarded as posts or parts of the net of a singles game. A return that passes under the net cord between the singles sticks and adjacent doubles post without touching either net cord, net or doubles post and falls within the court, is a good return.

25 **Hindrance of a Player** In case a player is hindered in making a stroke by anything not within his control, except a permanent fixture of the Court, or except as provided for in Rule 21, a let shall be called.

26 **Score in a Game** If a player wins his first point, the score is called 15 for that player; on winning his second point, the score is called 30 for that player; on winning his third point, the score is called 40 for that player, and the fourth point won by a player is scored game for that player except as below:-
If both players have won three points, the score is called deuce; and the next point won by a player is scored advantage for that player. If the same player wins the next point, he wins the game; if the other

player wins the next point the score is again called deuce; and so on, until a player wins the two points immediately following the score at deuce, when the game is scored for that player.

27 Score in a Set (a) A player (or players) who first wins six games wins a set; except that he must win by a margin of two games over his opponent and where necessary a set shall be extended until this margin is achieved.

(b) The tie-break system of scoring may be adopted as an alternative to the advantage set system in paragraph (a) of this Rule provided the decision is announced in advance of the match.

In this case, the following Rules shall be effective:
The tie-break shall operate when the score reaches six games all in any set except in the third or fifth set of a three set or five set match respectively when an ordinary advantage set shall be played, unless otherwise decided and announced in advance of the match.
The following system shall be used in a tie-break game.

Singles
(i) A player who first wins seven points shall win the game and the set provided he leads by a margin of two points. If the score reaches six points all the game shall be extended until this margin has been achieved. Numerical scoring shall be used throughout the tie-break game.

(ii) The player whose turn it is to serve shall be the Server for the first point. His opponent shall be the Server for the second and third points and thereafter each player shall serve alternately for two consecutive points until the winner of the game and set has been decided. (iii) From the first point, each service shall be delivered alternately from the right and left Courts, beginning from the right Court. If service from a wrong half of the Court occurs and is undetected, all play resulting from such wrong service or services shall stand, but the inaccuracy of station shall be corrected immediately it is discovered.

(iv) Players shall change ends after every six points and at the conclusion of the tie-break game.

(v) The tie-break game shall count as one game for the ball change, except that, if the balls are due to be changed at the beginning of the tie-break, the change shall be delayed until the second game of the following set.

Doubles
In doubles the procedure for singles shall apply. The player whose turn it is to serve shall be the Server for the first point. Thereafter each player shall serve in rotation for two points, in the same order as previously in that set, until the winners of the game and set have been decided.

Rotation of Service
The player (or pair in the case of doubles) who served first in the tie-break game shall receive service in the first game of the following set.

28 Maximum Number of Sets The maximum number of sets in a match shall be 5, or where women take part, 3.

29 Role of Court Officials In matches where an Umpire is appointed, his decision shall be final; but where a Referee is appointed, an appeal shall lie to him from the decision of an Umpire on a question of law, and in all such cases the decision of the Referee shall be final.

In matches where assistants to the Umpire are appointed (Linesmen, Net-cord Judges, Foot-fault Judges) their decisions shall be final on questions of fact except that if in the opinion of an Umpire a clear mistake has been made he shall have the right to change the decision of an assistant or order a let to be played. When such an assistant is unable to give a decision he shall indicate this immediately to the Umpire who shall give a decision. When an Umpire is unable to give a decision on a question of fact he shall order a let to be played.

In *Davis Cup* matches or other team competitions where a Referee is on Court, any decision can be changed by the Referee, who may also instruct an Umpire to order a let to be played.
The Referee, in his discretion, may at any time postpone a match on account of darkness or the condition of the ground or the weather. In any case of postponement the previous score and previous occupancy of Courts shall hold good, unless the Referee and the players unanimously agree otherwise.

30 Continuous Play & Rest Periods Play shall be continuous from the first service until the match is concluded, in accordance with the following provisions:
(a) If the first service is a fault, the second service must be struck by the Server without delay.

The Receiver must play to the reasonable pace of the Server and must be ready to receive when the Server is ready to serve. When changing ends a maximum of one minute thirty seconds shall elapse from the moment the ball goes out of play at the end of the game to the time the ball is struck for the first point of the next game. The Umpire shall use his discretion when there is interference which makes it impractical for play to be continuous.

The organizers of international circuits and team events recognized by the ITF may determine the time allowed between points, which shall not at any time exceed 25 seconds.
(b) Play shall never be suspended, delayed or interfered with for the purpose of enabling a player to recover his strength, breath, or physical condition. However, in the case of accidental injury, the Umpire may allow a one-time three minute suspension for that injury.

The organizers of international circuits and team events recognized by the ITF may extend the one-time suspension period from three minutes to five minutes.
(c) If, through circumstances outside the control of the player, his clothing, footwear or equipment (excluding racket) becomes out of adjustment in such a way that it is impossible or undesirable for him to play on, the Umpire may suspend play while the maladjustment is rectified.
(d) The Umpire may suspend or delay play at any time as may be necessary and appropriate.
(e) After the third set, or when women take part the second set, either player is entitled to a rest, which shall not exceed 10 minutes, or in countries situated between

latitude 15 degrees north and latitude 15 degrees south, 45 minutes and furthermore, when necessitated by circumstances not within the control of the players, the Umpire may suspend play for such a period as he may consider necessary. If play is suspended and is not resumed until a later day the rest may be taken only after the third set (or when women take part the second set) of play on such a later day, competition of an unfinished set being counted as one set. If play is suspended and is not resumed until 10 min-utes have elapsed in the same day the rest may be taken only after three consecutive sets have been played without interruption (or when women take part two sets), completion of an unfinished set being counted as one set.

Any nation and/or committee organizing a tournament, match or competition, other than the International Tennis Championships (*Davis Cup* and *Federation Cup*), is at liberty to modify this provision or omit it from its regulations provided this is announced before the event commences.

(f) A tournament committee has the discretion to decide the time allowed for a warm-up period prior to a match but this may not exceed five minutes and must be announced before the event commences.

(g) When approved point penalty and non-accumulative point penalty systems are in operation, the Umpire shall make his decisions within the terms of those systems.

(h) Upon violation of the principle that play shall be continuous the Umpire may, after giving due warning, disqualify the offender.

31 Coaching During the playing of a match in a team competition, a player may receive coaching from a captain who is sitting on the court only when he changes ends at the end of a game, but not when he changes ends during a tie-break game. A player may not receive coaching during the playing of any other match. The provisions of this rule must be strictly construed. After due warning an offending player may be disqualified. When an approved point penalty system is in operation, the Umpire shall impose penalties according to that system.
Note: The word "coaching" includes any advice or instruction.

32 Changing Balls In cases where balls are to be changed after a specified number of games, if the balls are not changed in the correct sequence, the mistake shall be corrected when the player, or pair in the case of doubles, who should have served with new balls is next due to serve. Thereafter the balls shall be changed so that the numnber of games between changes shall be that originally agreed.

DOUBLES RULES

33 The Doubles Game The above Rules shall apply to the Doubles Game except as below.

34 The Doubles Court For the Doubles Game, the Court shall be 10.97m (36ft) in width, i.e. 1.37m (4½in) wider on each side than the Court for the Singles Game, and those portions of the singles side-lines which lie between the two service-lines shall be called the service side-lines. In other respects, the Court shall be similar to that described in Rule 1, but the portions of the singles side-lines between the base-line and service-line on each side of the net may be omitted if desired.

35 Order of Service in Doubles The order of serving shall be decided at the beginning of each set as follows:- The pair who have to serve in the first game of each set shall decide which partner shall do so and the opposing pair shall decide similarly for the second game. The partner of the player who served in the first game shall serve in the third; the partner of the player who served in the second game shall serve in the fourth, and so on in the same order in all the subsequent games of a set.

36 Order of Receiving in Doubles The order of receiving the service shall be decided at the beginning of each set as follows:-

The pair who have to receive the service in the first game shall decide which partner shall receive the first service, and that partner shall continue to receive the first service in every odd game throughout that set. The opposing pair shall likewise decide which partner shall receive the first service in the second game and that partner shall continue to receive the first service in every even game throughout that set. Partners shall receive the service alternately throughout each game.

37 Service Out of Turn in Doubles If a partner serves out of his turn, the partner who ought to have served shall serve as soon as the mistake is discovered, but all points scored, and any faults served before such discovery, shall be reckoned. If a game shall have been completed before such discovery, the order of service remains as altered.

38 Error in Order of Receiving in Doubles If during a game the order of receiving the service is changed by the Receivers it shall remain as altered until the end of the game in which the mistake is discovered, but the partners shall resume their original order of receiving in the next game of that set in which they are Receivers of the service.

39 Service Fault in Doubles The service is a fault as provided for by Rule 10, or if the ball touches the Server's partner or anything which he wears or carries; but if the ball served touches the partner of the Receiver, or anything which he wears or carries, not being a let under Rule 14 (a) before it hits the ground, the Server wins the point.

40 Playing the Ball in Doubles The ball shall be struck alternately by one or other player of the opposing pairs, and if a player touches the ball in play with his racket in contravention of this Rule, his opponents win the point.

Note: Except where otherwise stated, every reference in these Rules to the masculine includes the feminine gender.

INDEX

ACKNOWLEDGEMENTS

I would very much like to thank Abdul Rahman Hariri and Micheline Diegan for the photography in this book. Also Toni Barlow for all his work in the compilation of the first draft, Helen Van Wagenen, Bill Angus and Helen Keith for the proof reading of the final draft. Many thanks to Paul A. Lubbers, Ph.D, Director of Coaching Education, USTA Player Development, for allowing me to use photos from the USTA 'High-Performance Coaching' newsletters.

A big thankyou to Sami Parbhoo and Manuel Hirezi for their work on the front and back covers and Miranda Conyers for help on the computer. Thankyou to my loving parents for all the support when developing my tennis in the junior days and putting me through college. A special thankyou to my good friends Robert Warren back in England and Robert Grow in the States who really helped me develop as a player and trainer. Don't let me forget the children who appear in the group progression shots who demonstrated tremendous patience during the photo shoots in the intense Abu Dhabi heat. Also a big thankyou to Khalid Al Ameri for his help with the individual progression shots. This book is dedicated to my good friend and former regular practice partner from my college days Hugh Wauchope who lost his life at far too young an age.

For any information or questions regarding "Coaching and Learning Tennis Basics" please contact Patrick Diegan at www.Diegan@bellsouth.net

Other useful websites include the following. All have links to other sites that may be more specific to your needs.

www.PTRtenis.org
www.USTA.com
www.USAtennisflorida.com
www.ATPtennis.com
www.WTAtour.com
www.ITFtennis.com
www.USPTA.com
www.TennisWarehouse.com
www.1stserve.com

Printed in the United States
144927LV00002B/184/A